THE PARENTHOOD ADVANTAGE

THE PARENTHOOD ADVANTAGE

Building Corporate Cultures That Value Working Parents

Mason Donovan *and* Mark Kaplan

Published by DG Press
PO Box 172
Salisbury, NH 03268
Tel: 603-393-0335
www.TheDagobaGroup.com

Printed in the United States of America

ISBN: 978-1-7327262-7-7

CONTENTS

ACKNOWLEDGEMENTS

Although our names are listed as the authors of this book, it feels disingenuous to call it solely "our book." This work was nourished, inspired, and created by so many.

First, our thanks—and perhaps an apology—go to all the individuals we approached in children's bookstores, on airplanes, in parks, and everywhere in between. If we overheard your conversation about parenthood, or saw you with a child or expecting one, we unabashedly asked about your experience as a working parent. Without exception, you gave us your time and your thoughts.

We are equally grateful to our clients, friends, and colleagues who joined us for more formal conversations—whether scheduled Zoom interviews or thoughtful exchanges that informed our ideas and shaped this book. It has been a true privilege to share part of your story. While your identities have been kept confidential, as promised, many of you will recognize yourselves in the stories and examples throughout these pages.

We also owe deep gratitude to our friends and family who gave us respite and space to write while we cared for two infants. A particular thank-you goes to our family members Jim, Maria, and Debbie for carrying so much of the load in those early months and beyond. To our nanny, Tracy, whose steady care provided balance and peace of mind, we are profoundly grateful.

On the book creation side, we thank our editor Susan and our cover designer Mark, who have been with us across publishers and projects. To our first publisher and continuous supporter, we thank Jill for her excellent guidance. We also welcomed new members to the team for this book—our publicist Lissa and type-setter Jamie—whose expertise helped bring this manuscript into the world. We are grateful to our advance readers who provided their time and thoughts that helped us polish this final edition.

Writing this book has made us stronger both as professionals and as parents because of all that was shared with us. And lastly, although this book is rooted in our decades of work in inclusion and wellness, its deepest inspiration comes from our children, Adiran and Iyla. While we conducted extensive research and hundreds of conversations, we did not need to look further than our own lives to realize that becoming parents has made us stronger in every facet of life.

To all who contributed—thank you.

INTRODUCTION

It was a lazy Sunday morning, the kind where the world feels temporarily paused. A steaming cup of tea sat half drunk on the counter. The dog, oblivious to any impending chaos, stretched lazily in a patch of sunlight on the floor. The house was quiet, save for the occasional ping of a phone notification. It was the kind of morning where the biggest decision I planned to make was whether to have breakfast at home or go out.

Then, at 8 a.m., our world stopped.

A text message from our doctor cut through the calm like a lightning strike: "She's in labor. Six weeks early."

Six weeks. That wasn't a margin of error—it was an entirely different timeline.

Mark had just landed in Las Vegas for his father's birthday after a business trip to London. Mason was at home, still out walking the dog. And our surrogate—carrying the child we had planned for so meticulously—was thousands of miles away, in a hospital bed, her body deciding that now was the time.

Panic surges in moments like these, but so does adrenaline. We booked our flights within minutes, and we quickly condensed our carefully crafted checklist, cutting it to a six-hour sprint (we'd originally planned a leisurely departure a full month before the due date). The dog had to be cared for—thank you, Sarah! The house, still bracing for winter in New Hampshire, needed to be winterized and watched. The nursery, a woodland-themed haven painstakingly designed over months, sat empty, waiting for our child to arrive. And while the baby's bag—packed two months in advance with every possible newborn essential—was ready to go, ours were not.

There's a strange shift in the mind when you enter crisis mode. The normal rhythms of decision making collapse, replaced by rapid-fire triage. What is necessary? What is urgent? What can be left behind? Within hours, Mason was racing to the airport, luggage hastily packed, boarding a last-minute flight. Mark, still in Las Vegas, scrambled to reroute himself. The plan was clear: Mason would arrive that night, and Mark the next day.

Then came the next twist in the story.

Midflight, as Mason crossed time zones at thirty-five thousand feet, a new message came in: the contractions had slowed. There was a chance we might have days, maybe even weeks. It was a breath of relief, but one laced with uncertainty. This was no longer just about getting there; it was about preparing for the unknown.

Landing at the airport, Mason's first challenge wasn't the hospital—it was finding a place to stay. The Airbnb, booked in advance, was abruptly canceled by the host while Mason was waiting for his luggage. Now, in a city he barely knew, he scrambled to secure a hotel for at least the next few nights. By the time his head hit the pillow that night, exhaustion had fully settled in.

And then, at 10:00 p.m., the final text came.

"Emergency C-section scheduled for 5:00 a.m. Baby will be in the NICU."

No time to process, no time to plan. Just action.

At 5:15 a.m., our son came into the world, and within moments, he was whisked away to the neonatal intensive care unit, hooked up to wires and tubes, his tiny body fighting to adjust to life outside the womb.

And suddenly, nothing else mattered.

For the next four weeks, life existed within the walls of the neonatal intensive care unit (NICU). The business we had spent years building? It disappeared from our minds. Deadlines, emails, client meetings—they all faded into the background. Every ounce of energy was devoted to the fragile human being who now defined our world. We arrived every morning at eight o'clock when the hospital doors opened, and we stayed until eight at night, when the nurses, with gentle but firm insistence, reminded us that we had to leave. Those hours outside the hospital felt like liminal space, like we had pressed a pause button on life itself.

We had expected exhaustion, but nothing could have prepared us for the total emotional surrender we experienced in those weeks. The fear. The hope. The constant dance between helplessness and determination. The way time moved strangely, at once too fast and too slow.

And yet, within this chaos, something else happened.

Between the twelve-hour hospital visits and whispered conversations over plastic coffee cups, we started hearing stories. From doctors. From nurses. From clients and colleagues who reached out with messages of support. There were stories of other parents. Stories of juggling careers and caregiving. Of trying—and failing—to balance work with the unpredictable nature of new life. They were stories of guilt, exhaustion, and the unspoken expectation that parents, particularly mothers, had to choose between ambition and family.

It was in those conversations that we began to see the larger picture.

Because while our story was unique—surrogacy, a premature birth, an emergency transcontinental sprint—it was also universal. Every working parent, in some form or another, faces a moment when their professional world collides with the inescapable reality of parenthood, a moment when they realize that, despite all the preparation in the world, they were never truly ready.

And yet, there is no guidebook.

Companies have policies, but they often lack structure and consistency in the policies and the way they are applied. Employers offer leave, but not support. Parents are left to figure out the balance on their own, navigating the push and pull of professional ambition and personal responsibility with little more than trial and error.

Sitting in that hospital room, watching our son fight for every breath, we understood something with profound clarity: this was more than our story. This was a conversation that needed to happen.

The Workplace Wake-Up Call

In the weeks that followed our son's birth, life became a study in contrasts. Inside the NICU, time slowed to a crawl—every breath, every beep of a monitor, every doctor's update felt monumental. Outside, the world we once controlled through calendars and deadlines raced ahead without us. Emails piled up, client meetings came and went, apologies were sent. Some obligations simply slipped through the cracks.

Yet in those brief moments when we resurfaced—checking in with work between feedings, glancing at emails in the quiet of a waiting room—we saw the disconnect. The world of work wasn't designed for this.

Before parenthood, we had worked closely with companies on inclusion and workplace wellness. We understood the systems that privileged some people and sidelined others. We had heard the stories of parents struggling to balance career ambition with caregiving demands. But now, for the first time, we were living it . . . a meeting scheduled for 7:30 p.m., right when the baby needed to be fed . . . a conference that required travel, but no realistic way to leave home . . . an unspoken shift in perception, where colleagues, without discussion, began assuming we were too "distracted" for leadership opportunities. Before, we had listened to these frustrations from clients. Now, we felt them in our bones. And we weren't alone.

The more we listened, the more we saw the hidden fractures in corporate culture.

The workplace was built on an outdated assumption: that employees exist in a steady state. That their ambition, availability, and productivity are constant over time. That personal lives don't interfere with professional lives.

But real life isn't steady.

Parenthood is not a disruption—it's an evolution. It reshapes priorities, identities, and skills. It doesn't make employees less valuable—it makes them more adaptable, more efficient, more empathetic, more capable. And yet, most workplaces still haven't figured out how to see that, let alone support it.

Sitting in the NICU, between tube feedings and doctors' rounds, we kept coming back to the same questions:

Why isn't there a structured approach to navigating work as an expectant parent?

Why don't companies provide real guidance—not just policies, but a framework for preparing for leave, transitioning back, and ensuring careers stay on track?

Why do we treat parenthood as a temporary or sometimes a permanent setback instead of recognizing it as a natural and valuable part of professional growth?

And, perhaps most importantly: What would it take to change this?

That's where this book begins.

The Systemic Challenge: Why This Book Matters

There's a familiar pattern in the way workplaces handle parenthood.

At first, there's celebration: the birth announcement, the warm congratulations, the company-wide email from a manager saying, "We're so happy for you!" Maybe there's even a baby shower, a round of well-wishes, a moment when it feels like the workplace is ready to embrace this new chapter with you.

Then comes the shift.

It happens quietly. Meetings are scheduled without you. High-profile projects go to others. Not because you've asked for less responsibility, but because someone assumes you'd prefer it that way. Your boss assures you that everything will be fine while you're out, but beneath the surface, you wonder if your absence is quietly reshaping your future.

Then comes the return.

You walk back through the office doors (or log into your first meeting after leave) and realize that, while your job is technically the same, nothing feels familiar. People ask how the baby is doing but few ask how *you* are doing. You try to dive back in, but the momentum you once had seems to have shifted. And somewhere along the way, your ambition came to be measured not by your performance but by an assumed set of priorities, ones you didn't choose.

"She's probably not looking for a promotion right now."

"He's got his hands full at home."

"Let's not overwhelm them—it's a lot coming back from leave."

And just like that, careers are quietly rerouted.

We've seen this too many times in our professional lives. And in the hundreds of interviews we conducted while writing this book, we heard it regularly.

Then there were the companies that genuinely wanted to support working parents but had no idea how to do it effectively. Because that's the real issue: it's not just that workplaces fail parents, it's that they don't even realize they're failing them.

Many companies tout their support for working parents, yet a gap persists between policy and lived experience. Parenthood is still seen as a professional liability, despite the fact that it builds precisely the skills today's workplaces value most—resilience, prioritization, emotional intelligence, and adaptability. This book challenges outdated assumptions and makes the case that parenthood isn't a detour from professional growth—it's an advantage. We'll explore how and why that's true in the chapters ahead. This isn't just a social argument. It's a business argument.

What to Expect in This Book

For decades, workplaces have struggled to integrate parenthood into their cultures. Policies exist, but many fall short. Parents return from leave only to find their career trajectories altered in ways they never anticipated. Nonparents feel the strain of carrying the additional workload. And companies, despite good intentions, often fail to realize where they're falling short.

This book isn't just about identifying those gaps—it's about closing them. We wrote this book with an understanding that the people who need it most often have the least time to spare. That's why it's not meant only to be read cover to cover in a linear fashion. We invite you to start with the chapters that resonate most with your experience or current questions.

Each chapter stands on its own, with intentional overlap in key themes. This allows you to engage with the content at your own pace, in whatever order feels most useful—without losing the thread.

We begin with Chapter 1, "Evolutions," exploring how both parental leave and the identity of new parents have transformed over time. This foundational chapter frames the discussions to come, illustrating the three key phases of transition that working parents experience.

From there, Chapter 2, "Embracing Parents in the Workplace: The Business Case," presents a compelling argument for why companies should care about the parents in their workforce—not just from a moral standpoint but from a business strategy perspective. Companies that support working parents retain talent, build stronger teams, and drive innovation.

Chapter 3, "Penalties and Bonuses," unpacks the unconscious biases surrounding working parents—the penalties mothers often face, the quiet career stagnation for fathers who take paternity leave, and the advantages granted to those who conform to traditional workplace norms.

Beyond external workplace challenges, parenthood itself is an internal transformation. Chapter 4, "The Psychological Shift to

Parenthood," helps managers understand how employees change on a fundamental level—mentally, emotionally, and even cognitively—when they become parents. This shift, while deeply personal, also impacts the way parents engage at work.

Building on that shift, Chapter 5, "Boundaries and Balance," explores the tension between work and home life, helping managers and employees alike create structures that prevent burnout and foster sustainable careers.

Identity is at the heart of professional growth, and Chapter 6, "Redefining Identity and Purpose," highlights how parenthood reshapes priorities, strengthens purpose, and often deepens commitment to meaningful work.

In many ways, parenthood is leadership training in disguise. Chapter 7, "The Developmental Journey," makes the case that parenting sharpens key professional skills—including crisis management, decision making, and prioritization—turning working parents into more effective leaders.

But for all the philosophical and cultural shifts needed, there are also logistics to manage. Chapter 8, "Navigating Logistics," is a practical guide, offering clear strategies for employees and managers on preparing for leave, ensuring seamless transitions, and supporting a successful return.

Finally, we zoom out to the big picture in Chapter 9, "The Corporate Role." This chapter examines how companies can move beyond small policy adjustments and build a workplace culture that sees parenthood as an advantage rather than a burden.

This book is more than a discussion. It's a call to action—for managers, leaders, and employees who want to create workplaces that don't just accommodate parents but use their strengths to advantage, creating a stronger, more resilient workforce for the future.

The companies that stop sidelining working parents and start leveraging their strengths will be the ones that thrive—retaining talent, building resilient teams, and creating cultures rooted in loyalty and long-term performance. This book is about shifting the conversation: parenthood at work is not a liability; it's a training ground for emotional intelligence and leadership. In 2024, the U.S. Surgeon General warned that parental stress had become a public health crisis, yet many companies continue to treat it as a private matter. The truth is, rigid schedules, poor leave policies, and outdated workplace expectations directly contribute to burnout and attrition. Supporting parents isn't just about doing the right thing—it's about building stronger businesses. Companies that embrace this reality see better retention, stronger teams, and more sustainable growth. The data is clear, the need is urgent, and the question is no longer whether to change—but whether companies will lead the way or be left behind.

This book is not primarily about making a moral argument. It's about making a business case—one that proves that integrating parenthood into the workplace isn't just the right thing to do; it's the smart thing to do.

The workplace is changing. The only question is: Will your company evolve with it or be left behind?

1 | EVOLUTIONS

Parenthood is an evolution, both personal and societal. It transforms individuals in profound and unpredictable ways, reshaping priorities, identities, and daily rhythms. But just as no parent remains unchanged by the arrival of a child, no society remains static in its approach to supporting those who take on the essential roles of having and raising children. The way we define, experience, and support new parents—especially in the workplace—has been in constant motion for generations. Underlying what has been a bevy of policy and legislative changes, particularly over the last fifty years, is a shift in attitudes about parenthood, gender roles, and the role of institutions both public and private.

It is impossible to speak about the evolution of parenthood without also speaking about the evolution of gender stereotypes and gender roles. Between the 1970s and the 2010s, attitudes toward women's roles as mothers and support for their equality in the workplace have grown substantially more progressive. Alongside the increase in support for women's freedom are changes in attitudes about the role of men. In short, men are increasingly interested in having a more encompassing and active role as parents. Additionally, changing societal attitudes support this expanded role for men. These changes in attitudes about the roles of men and women have led directly to an evolving view of the family and the relationship between parents/families and the workplace. These sorts of cultural and attitudinal shifts almost always result in legislative and policy changes.

Parental leave, once nonexistent, then a privilege afforded to few, and now a structured (though still uneven) benefit, reflects this evolution, at least to some extent. As of March 2023, only 27 percent of civilian workers in the United States have access to paid family leave, while 90 percent have access to unpaid family leave. Access to paid family leave is particularly limited among lower-wage workers; for instance, among the lowest 10 percent of earners, only about 5 percent have access to paid family leave. These disparities highlight the ongoing challenges in making parental leave policies more inclusive and supportive for all workers. Over time, what was once solely maternity leave has grown to include paternity leave, parental leave, and even caregiver leave, adapting to the realities of modern families. Yet, for many working parents, these policies still feel like a patchwork—essential but often insufficient, offering time but not always support, permission but not always acceptance. Family-related laws and policies are still evolving.

At the same time, the personal journey of becoming a parent is its own evolution, one that unfolds in a series of transformations both subtle and seismic. From the moment of birth through the first six months and beyond, a new parent's life is in constant motion. Sleep patterns, relationships, professional identities, and self-perception all shift under the weight of this new responsibility. The skills that once defined a person's success at work—organization, leadership, crisis management—take on new meaning in the context of a newborn, while entirely new skills emerge, forged in the fires of exhaustion and unconditional love.

This chapter explores both these evolutions: the historical shifts in the way parental leave has been defined and implemented, and the deeply personal transformation that occurs in the first months of parenthood. Understanding where we have been, both as individuals and as a society, provides a foundation for navigating what's ahead. For new parents, this chapter offers insight into the changes—practical, emotional, and professional—that accompany the transition to parenthood. For managers, employers, policymakers, and advocates, it serves as a reminder that just as parents must evolve, so too must the systems that support them.

The early months of parenthood are all about adaptation. The same could be said for the world of work. And as both continue to evolve, one truth remains: the more we recognize and support the profound transformation of becoming a parent, the stronger our families, workplaces, and societies will be.

The evolution of parental leave is a vast and complex story, one that could fill an entire book on its own. While this chapter doesn't take a deep historical dive, it provides an overview of how parental leave has transformed over time. Understanding where we started, the progress we've made, and the gaps that remain offer important context for today's working parents, their companies, and the road ahead.

Parental Leave: A Chronological Perspective

Parental leave has undergone a remarkable evolution over the past century, reflecting profound changes in societal values, workforce dynamics, and family structures. From its earliest iteration as a safeguard for women's health to its modern form encompassing gender-neutral policies and caregiver support, parental leave has become a cornerstone of workplace equity and family well-being. This chapter explores its historical journey, tracing the origins, legislative milestones, and cultural shifts that have shaped today's policies on leave.

Industrialization and Early Labor Protections (1800s–1930s)

The rise of industrialization in the nineteenth century marked the beginning of formal employment for women outside of domestic roles. Factory jobs subjected women to hazardous conditions, long hours, and physically demanding labor. Pregnancy was often viewed as an impediment, and without any protections, many women were dismissed once they could no longer perform their duties.

In response, early labor reforms in Europe, particularly in Germany, laid the groundwork for maternity protections. In 1883, Germany introduced a groundbreaking social insurance program under Otto von Bismarck, offering financial support to women post-childbirth. Other European nations, including France and Sweden, followed suit, acknowledging that protecting maternal health was not only a moral imperative but also an economic necessity for sustaining a stable workforce.

In the United States, however, progress was slow. The Progressive Era (1890s–1920s) saw labor reform movements advocating for better working conditions for women and children, but maternity leave remained an elusive goal. Women were often expected to leave the workforce entirely upon pregnancy, reinforcing traditional gender roles. The U.S. passed the Wagner Act in 1935 which protected the rights of employees to unionize and further fight for working mothers and, almost a century later, working fathers.

The Changing Role of Women in the Workforce (1940s–1950s)
The onset of World War II in the 1940s dramatically altered women's participation in the workforce. Though some women, particularly poorer women, had always worked outside the home, with men off at war, women took on new roles in factories, offices, and other essential industries, demonstrating their capabilities in professional environments that had traditionally been dominated by men. The image of "Rosie the Riveter" symbolized women's vital contributions to the economy.

To support working mothers, some employers introduced basic maternity benefits, although these were largely informal and inconsistent. The postwar era saw a push to return women to domestic roles, but many had become permanent members of the workforce, setting the stage for future discussions about maternity leave as a necessary employment policy.

The Emergence of Maternity Leave (1960s–1970s)
By the 1960s, more women were pursuing careers alongside motherhood, creating an urgent need for workplace protections. In the absence of federal mandates, short-term disability insurance became the primary mechanism for maternity leave in the

United States. Employers allowed pregnancy to be classified as a temporary disability, enabling women to receive some income while recovering from childbirth. This model, however, framed maternity leave as a medical issue rather than a family necessity or an individual preference.

The women's liberation movement of the 1970s brought workplace gender discrimination into sharp focus. Activists demanded stronger policies to protect pregnant workers, arguing that short-term disability insurance was insufficient. The passage of the Pregnancy Discrimination Act in 1978 was a pivotal moment, as the law prohibited employers from firing or penalizing employees for pregnancy-related conditions. While this act reinforced workplace protections, it did not mandate paid maternity leave, meaning that many women were left vulnerable.

The Shift Toward Gender-Inclusive Leave (1980s–1990s)

The 1980s and 1990s saw increasing recognition of fathers' roles in caregiving. Scandinavian countries led the charge, with Sweden pioneering gender-neutral parental leave policies in 1974. These policies allowed both parents to take time off, encouraging a shift in traditional caregiving responsibilities.

In contrast, the United States lagged behind. The Family and Medical Leave Act (FMLA) of 1993 provided a major breakthrough, granting up to twelve weeks of unpaid, job-protected leave for qualifying employees. While this law applied to both mothers and fathers, its unpaid nature meant that many workers, particularly those in low-income jobs, could not afford to take advantage of it.

Nevertheless, FMLA was the first federal acknowledgment that parental leave should not be limited to mothers. It opened the door to further advocacy for paid leave and a more equitable division of caregiving responsibilities.

Expanding Parental Leave (2000s–2010s)

As family structures diversified, so too did the understanding of parental leave. The rise of same-sex parenting, adoption, and nonbirth parents created a demand for more inclusive leave policies. Some progressive companies began offering paid parental leave, recognizing its benefits for employee retention and workplace morale.

Meanwhile, certain U.S. states took the lead in implementing paid leave programs. California launched the first paid family leave initiative in 2004, followed by states including New York, Washington, and Massachusetts in the following years. These programs provided partial wage replacement for employees taking time off to care for a new child or a sick family member.

By the late 2010s, major corporations, particularly in the tech industry, were competing to offer the most generous parental leave benefits. Companies such as Google, Facebook, and Netflix set new standards by providing extended paid leave to both mothers and fathers, normalizing the expectation that all parents, regardless of gender, should have time to bond with their children.

The Modern Landscape and Future of Parental Leave (2020s and Beyond)

The COVID-19 pandemic in 2020 further underscored the need for robust parental leave policies. With schools and childcare centers closed, many parents struggled to balance work and caregiving responsibilities. Governments and businesses were forced to reevaluate existing leave policies, leading to expanded paid leave benefits in several industries.

Today, parental leave continues to evolve, with an increasing emphasis on gender neutrality, paid leave expansion, and flexibility. Countries like Sweden and Canada have set global benchmarks, offering extensive paid parental leave with provisions for both parents. In the U.S., federal paid leave remains a topic of debate, with ongoing advocacy for a national policy that ensures equitable access for all workers. States have been carving out legislation where federal law is lacking. For example, in 2025, New York State was the first in the nation to enact a law requiring employers to provide twenty hours of paid leave as a stand-alone benefit for pregnant workers so they could attend their prenatal health-care visits.

As the workforce becomes more diverse and the traditional family model shifts, the future of parental leave will likely emphasize flexibility, allowing parents to choose how and when to take leave in ways that best support their unique circumstances. The integration of remote-work and hybrid-work models may further shape how leave policies are designed and implemented.

The Language of Leave

As leave policies have evolved, so has the terminology. Following are some key terms used throughout this chapter and beyond.

• **Parental leave:** A gender-neutral term for leave taken by any parent—biological, adoptive, or otherwise.

• **Maternity leave:** Leave specifically designated for mothers during and after childbirth. The assumption in most firms that use this term is that it is for the birthing mother. This can become confusing for a same-sex female couple or a couple that is utilizing surrogacy or an adoption. Maternity leave is often coupled with short-term disability if the company offers it.

• **Paternity leave:** Leave granted to fathers to support their partners and bond with their newborns or newly adopted children.

• **Bonding leave:** A period of leave focused on creating and strengthening the emotional connection between parents and their children. This leave is often applied for by fathers but is common for parents who adopt.

• **Primary and secondary caregivers:** The person primarily responsible for attending to the daily needs of a child or other dependent person, and the caregiver who provides support and respite, respectively. Corporations are now designating a primary caregiver because that person gets a longer leave. The company often allows an employee to be on their honor in determining their caregiver status. This distinction allows for nontraditional family roles.

• **Caregiver leave:** Leave taken to care for an aging, sick, or dependent family member, but can also be for the birth of a child.

• **Family and Medical Leave Act (FMLA):** A law that allows for up to twelve weeks of protected-job-status unpaid leave for, among other things, the birth or adoption of a child. This is sometimes the only type of leave available to employees.

• **Paid vs. unpaid leave:** A critical distinction determining whether employees receive financial compensation during leave.

Policy, Perception, and Parenthood

The evolution of parental leave reflects broader societal changes in gender roles, workforce participation, and family structures. From early maternity protections rooted in industrial labor reforms to the modern push for gender-inclusive and paid-leave policies, the journey has been one of progress and persistent advocacy. It is clear, however, that changing laws and policies don't always or quickly result in changing behavior, a reality we will discuss later in the book. So the process of change is both long and multifaceted, from institutions, government, employers, and individuals.

Deeply ingrained norms and stereotypes about parenthood and gender roles can create a lot of dissonance between what one *can* do (policies) and what one *should* do (behavior). While it is true that shifts in attitude generally precede and drive policy change, it is also true that policy change allows attitudinal shifts to be fully realized in behavior. Some research indicates that men and women wish to be even more egalitarian in their roles as parents, but they are limited by both uneven and insufficient policy support and a lingering perception that they will pay a career price. This desire among employees for more equal roles as parents represents an opportunity for organizations that wish to compete for talent.

As parental leave continues to adapt, ensuring universal access, financial support, and gender equity remains crucial. The future of parental leave must prioritize flexibility and inclusivity to support the needs of all families, ultimately contributing to a healthier and more equitable society, and to more effective organizations and institutions.

Just as parental leave has evolved to reflect changing societal norms, so too has the journey to becoming a parent. The transition to parenthood is not a single moment but an ongoing process, one that reshapes a person's identity, priorities, and daily life in profound ways. From the first sleepless nights to the delicate balance of returning to work, the early months of parenting are a period of continuous adaptation. Understanding this personal evolution is just as essential as understanding the policies that support it.

The Evolution of a New Parent's Life: From Birth to Six Months

Becoming a parent is one of the most profound transformations a person can undergo. The shift is immediate and all-encompassing, touching every aspect of life—physically, emotionally, psychologically, and professionally. While the arrival of a child is often envisioned as a moment of boundless joy, the reality is more complex. The first six months, in particular, are a period of constant adaptation, in which a parent's identity, priorities, and routines are in flux.

For working parents, especially those who take a temporary leave of two to three months before returning to their jobs, this evolution is layered with additional challenges. The transition from professional life to full-time caregiving and then back again requires not only logistical adjustments but also deep emotional and psychological recalibration. Parenthood introduces new constraints and opportunities, altering everything from time management and work–life boundaries to one's very sense of self.

The First Few Weeks: A New Reality Sets In

The early days after birth are marked by a seismic shift in daily life. Sleep deprivation reaches an intensity most new parents are unprepared for, as newborns wake every two to three hours around the clock to be fed, changed, and soothed. Time becomes fluid, with day and night blurring into an endless cycle of caregiving.

The physical toll on the birthing parent is substantial. For the birthing parent, the body is healing from a physically demanding process while simultaneously adjusting to hormonal fluctuations, postpartum bleeding, and the challenges of breastfeeding or bottle-feeding. Partners or nonbirth parents experience their own set of adjustments, including exhaustion, emotional recalibration, and a redefinition of their role in both parenting and household dynamics.

This period is also an emotional roller coaster. The joy of meeting one's child is often paired with moments of self-doubt, isolation, and, in some cases, postpartum mood disorders. The reality of round-the-clock care, the loss of personal autonomy, and the weight of new responsibilities can feel overwhelming. Even those who have thrived in high-pressure professional environments may find that newborn care presents an entirely different type of challenge. Your responses to the relentless unpredictability of your baby's needs—soothing inconsolable cries at two o'clock in the morning, fumbling through sleep-deprived days—represent a new kind of resilience.

For parents on leave, these first weeks are wholly immersive. The outside world fades as the immediate needs of the baby dictate every waking (and sleeping) moment. Many new parents describe this time as an alternate reality—one where their former selves, including their professional identities, feel distant or even irrelevant. The fast-paced, achievement-oriented mindset of the workplace is replaced by a world where productivity is measured not in emails answered or projects completed but in the small victories of keeping a newborn fed, clean, and comforted.

Months One to Three: Adapting to the Shifting Landscape

By the end of the first month, new parents begin to develop a tentative rhythm, though it is far from predictable. The baby may start showing early signs of social engagement, like making eye contact and responding to voices, offering parents their first glimpses of connection. These small but profound milestones provide emotional rewards that make the exhaustion more bearable.

Sleep remains a central challenge, as infants still wake frequently through the night, though some may begin to stretch their sleep in small increments. The unpredictability of infant sleep cycles means parents must develop strategies for rest and recovery, often taking shifts or learning to function on interrupted sleep.

For working parents who have taken two or three months of leave, this period carries the weight of an impending transition. As the return-to-work date approaches, parents must plan for childcare, navigate the logistics of feeding (whether pumping breast milk or transitioning to formula), and mentally prepare for the shift from full-time caregiving to a dual role as parent and professional.

Emotionally, this is a time of significant tension. Many parents experience anxiety, guilt, or even grief at the thought of leaving their baby, particularly if they feel they are just beginning to establish a routine. For those who have enjoyed their time on leave, the return to work can feel abrupt, as it forces them to shift from an emotionally immersive experience into a structured, results-driven environment.

At the same time, some parents look forward to reengaging with their professional identity. Work can provide a sense of normalcy, intellectual stimulation, and a break from the relentlessness of newborn care. However, even for those eager to return, the transition is not seamless. The demands of parenthood do not pause once the workday begins, and the mental load of managing both work and home life becomes an ongoing balancing act.

Months Three to Six: The New (Always Changing) Normal

Between three and six months, a baby's development accelerates. The baby gains better head control, begins to roll over, and develops an increased awareness of their surroundings. Sleep patterns continue to evolve—sometimes improving, sometimes regressing—keeping parents in a state of perpetual adjustment.

This phase marks a crucial transition for working parents. By this point, many have returned to their jobs, and are confronting the challenge of balancing work with caregiving. Managing a household with an infant requires meticulous planning. Morning routines must accommodate feedings, diaper changes, and daycare drop-offs. Evenings become a whirlwind of baby care, dinner preparation, and attempts to carve out time for personal or partner relationships.

For parents who are breastfeeding, pumping at work introduces another layer of complexity. This requires not only physical space and time but also mental energy, as many must navigate workplace policies and social dynamics around lactation breaks. Managers who ensure that the workplace provides flexible schedules and designated lactation spaces can significantly ease new parents' transition and improve long-term retention.

The mental load of parenthood remains immense. Beyond the physical demands of caring for an infant, there is constant cognitive strain—tracking feeding schedules, monitoring developmental milestones, coordinating childcare, and managing unexpected disruptions (such as illness, which can derail both work and home life).

For some parents, the workplace feels both familiar and foreign. Colleagues may welcome them back warmly, but the experience of parental leave often shifts one's perspective. The professional goals that once seemed paramount may now be viewed through a different lens. Some parents feel a renewed drive to excel at work, while others reset their priorities, questioning the traditional definitions of success.

The Continuous Evolution of Parenthood

After six months, the parent who first entered this journey is not the same person they were at the child's birth. They have undergone a profound transformation, not only in their daily routines but in their very sense of self. They have learned to function on less sleep, to pivot constantly, and to balance work and caregiving in ways they never imagined. The resilience and adaptability forged in this period are skills they will carry forward, both at home and in the workplace.

Yet, parenthood is not a journey with a fixed destination—it is an ongoing evolution. Just as a parent adapts to one phase, the next begins. The first six months are only the beginning, but they set a course for the way a working parent navigates the delicate and demanding balance of career and family in the years ahead.

The experience of evolving alongside a growing child is one of continual learning, adjustment, and self-discovery. With each passing month, parents refine their ability to anticipate, problem solve, and advocate for themselves and their families. The early struggles may fade into memory, but the skills and perspective gained during this time will remain, shaping both their personal and professional lives in ways that are lasting and meaningful.

Conclusion: The Intersection of Policy and Personal Evolution

The evolution of parental leave and the evolution of a new parent's life are deeply intertwined. One exists to support the other, yet as we've discussed, policies often lag behind the lived realities of working parents. While parental leave has expanded significantly, the personal transition into parenthood remains a profound and often challenging experience, one that extends far beyond the weeks or months a company may offer as leave.

For new parents, the early months are a master class in adaptability, resilience, and shifting priorities. For managers, their employees' transition to parenthood is not just about compliance with company policy—it's about the bigger picture of talent management and strategy. Leaders who champion parental support are likely improving their ability to retain and attract the best. These forward-thinking managers don't just build a more inclusive workplace, they create stronger, more resilient teams. A well-supported parent is not just a healthier, more engaged employee, they are a stronger leader, a sharper decision maker, and a more empathetic colleague. Companies that recognize the importance of this evolution, and structure their policies and cultures to support it, don't just improve retention and employee satisfaction, they build more resilient, high-performing organizations.

Parental leave is just the beginning. The real impact comes in how businesses choose to reintegrate, support, and empower working parents long after they return. In the next chapter, we'll explore the business case for investing in new parents—not just as a benefit, but as a strategic advantage.

Key Takeaways

- **Parental leave is a business strategy.** Strong parental policies improve retention, productivity, and talent attraction.
- **The first six months are critical.** Employees face major identity and logistical shifts; managerial support impacts engagement.
- **Culture matters as much as policy.** Many employees fear career penalties for taking leave. Leaders must normalize and support parental leave.
- **Parental support builds stronger teams.** Working parents develop resilience, adaptability, and leadership skills that benefit the workplace.

Reflection

1. Does your team feel safe using parental leave policies?
2. What biases about working parents exist in your organization?
3. How can you better support employees before, during, and after parental leave?
4. What business benefits could stronger parental policies bring to your company?

2 | EMBRACING PARENTS IN THE WORKPLACE: THE BUSINESS CASE

In 2013, a groundbreaking study from the Federal Reserve Bank of St. Louis set off a firestorm in corporate boardrooms.[1] The researchers examined the productivity levels of academics over the course of their careers, measuring research output at different life stages. The conclusion? Mothers—particularly those with two or more children—were significantly more productive than their counterparts without children. The data defied long-standing assumptions that parenthood diminishes workplace performance. Instead, it suggested the opposite: having children sharpened these professionals' ability to prioritize, multitask, and execute.

This finding is not an anomaly. A growing body of research reveals that parents—especially working mothers—develop skills that make them formidable employees. One study published in the *Journal of Applied Psychology* found that working parents exhibit higher levels of resilience, crisis management, and emotional intelligence, traits that are increasingly critical in today's fast-moving and uncertain business environment.[2]

Despite this evidence, corporate America continues to operate on outdated assumptions. According to a report by Lean In and McKinsey & Company, Mothers are often wrongly perceived as less committed to their jobs than women without children, based on the assumption that they can't fully invest in both work and family. This bias tends to deepen when mothers use flexible work arrangements, even if their performance matches that of their peers.[3] Fathers, meanwhile, are penalized when they take full parental leave, reinforcing an outdated model in which caregiving is seen as a liability rather than an asset.

These biases don't just harm employees; they cost businesses millions. Companies that fail to retain parents—especially women—face exorbitant turnover costs. Burnout, together with disengagement and lost institutional knowledge, add further financial strain. And yet, businesses that invest in parent-friendly policies—like Patagonia, which boasts a 100 percent retention rate among new mothers—consistently outperform their competitors.

The goal of this chapter is simple: to dismantle the myth that parents are "less than" employees and to reframe them as corporate assets. The data is clear—parents bring leadership qualities, adaptability, and efficiency that businesses need to stay competitive. The companies that recognize and harness this advantage will not only retain top talent but will also drive innovation, employee engagement, and long-term profitability.

In the pages ahead, we'll explore the economic and cultural forces shaping how businesses perceive parenthood. We'll look at real-world examples of companies that have embraced parents as a strategic advantage—and those that have paid the price for failing to do so. And, most importantly, we'll make the case that supporting employees who are parents is one of the smartest business decisions a company can make.

The ROI of Supporting Employees Who Are Parents

In 2015, a consulting firm quietly conducted an internal audit after noticing a troubling pattern. Highly talented midcareer employees—particularly women—were leaving at an alarming rate. The firm's leaders assumed that these employees were departing for more flexible roles or exiting the workforce entirely. But when they surveyed the employees, the leaders were stunned: these professionals weren't leaving because they wanted to work less. They were leaving because their employer had made it too difficult to stay.

This firm was not alone. According to research from the Center for Work-Life Policy, 43 percent of highly skilled women step away from their careers at some point, often due to workplace cultures that make balancing work and parenthood untenable.[4] The cost of replacing these employees is staggering. A study by the Work Institute estimates that replacing an employee costs employers approximately 33 percent of that employee's annual salary—and for senior roles, this number can be exponentially more due to recruitment, lost productivity, and training costs.[5]

But what if companies flipped the narrative? What if, instead of seeing parenthood as an obstacle, they saw it as an advantage? The numbers suggest that doing so isn't just an act of corporate goodwill—it's a financial imperative.

Retention and Reduced Turnover Costs

Supporting working parents isn't just a moral imperative—it's a proven strategy for increasing retention and reducing costly turnover. When thinking about how to reduce turnover among parents, recall Patagonia, the outdoor apparel company with an enviable 100 percent retention rate among new mothers. Their secret? A robust, family-friendly infrastructure that includes on-site childcare, paid parental leave, and flexible work arrangements. According to a *Harvard Business Review* analysis, Patagonia's childcare program pays for itself.[6] While many companies balk at the upfront costs, Patagonia found that retention savings, increased employee engagement, and reduced absenteeism more than offset the investment.

Contrast Patagonia's results with those of companies that fail to support working parents. Rigid workplace policies—such as inflexible scheduling and lack of remote options—are key contributors to employee turnover, particularly among those with caregiving responsibilities. When companies lose these employees, they don't just lose a worker—they lose institutional knowledge, client relationships, and the very leadership pipeline they've invested years in building.

And it's not just women who are leaving. A 2021 McKinsey & Company study revealed that fathers who take leave and experience workplace stigma are significantly more likely to quit than those who feel supported. In an era where talent is scarce, organizations that fail to accommodate parents will continue to hemorrhage their best people.

Productivity Gains from Parent Employees

The *Harvard Business Review* study on Patagonia's childcare program should have rewritten the narrative on working parents. One of the study's key findings was that parents develop an enhanced ability to triage tasks, prioritize ruthlessly, and eliminate inefficiencies. They don't have the luxury of wasting time in meetings that could have been emails, nor can they afford to get caught up in office politics. Instead, they get work done with laser focus.

According to a 2016 review by Joseph Grzywacz and Amy Smith, working parents often navigate complex and sustained stressors, which can foster greater resilience and cognitive flexibility over time—key components of adaptive thinking and effective problem-solving.[7] In industries that demand rapid decision making—such as finance, health care, and technology—these skills are invaluable.

Enhanced Employee Engagement and Loyalty

In 2019, the HR team at Microsoft conducted an internal analysis to understand the factors that contributed most to employee engagement and retention. The findings were unexpected: employees who felt that their employer actively supported their lives outside of work—including through parental leave, childcare benefits, and flexible schedules—were 45 percent more engaged and 30 percent more likely to stay with the company long term.

This isn't an isolated case. A Gallup poll found that engaged employees are 17 percent more productive and 21 percent more profitable for their organizations.[8] Meanwhile, a lack of engagement costs U.S. businesses a shocking $450 billion to $550 billion annually in lost productivity.

What does this mean for businesses? The companies that prioritize supporting parents create more engaged, productive, and loyal employees who drive better business outcomes.

The Numbers Don't Lie

• The Stanford Institute for Economic Policy Research found employees with flexible work arrangements were 13 percent more productive than those who did not.[9]

• Employees at companies with strong parental support programs report more loyalty and commitment, leading to higher retention rates. (Boston Consulting Group)[10]

• Firms that invest in on-site childcare or childcare stipends see a return on investment ranging from 90 to 425 percent, driven by higher retention, increased productivity, and reduced absenteeism, according to a 2024 analysis by Boston Consulting Group.[11]

• Generous parental leave policies are associated with higher female labor force participation and leadership representation, as countries with more supportive leave frameworks tend to see more women advancing into senior roles (World Economic Forum).[12]

Companies that embrace working parents gain a more resilient, efficient, and engaged workforce, while those that ignore the needs of parents pay the price in attrition, burnout, and lost productivity. The business case is clear: supporting parent employees is a strategic advantage.

Up next, we'll explore why parenthood is one of the most effective leadership incubators that organizations have at their disposal.

Why Emotionally Intelligent Leaders Win

In 2018, Google launched a research initiative called Project Oxygen to determine what made their best managers excel. The conclusion was unexpected. The most effective leaders weren't those with the highest IQs or the deepest technical expertise. Instead, they were those who demonstrated high emotional intelligence—leaders who could listen, empathize, and build trust with their teams.

Parenthood, as it turns out, is one of the most rigorous training grounds for emotional intelligence. A study published in *The Journal of Vocational Behavior* found that employees with children exhibited significantly higher levels of emotional intelligence.[13] The reason is simple: parents spend years developing patience, as well as active-listening and conflict-mediation skills, all of which are essential for effective leadership.

Salesforce CEO Marc Benioff has spoken openly about the importance of emotional intelligence in leadership, arguing that the best executives aren't just analytically sharp, they are deeply empathetic, strong communicators, and able to inspire trust. He credits much of his company's success to the fact that his leadership team is filled with individuals who understand how to manage people with care—a skill set honed through parenting.

The business case for emotionally intelligent leadership is strong. Research published in *The Secured Lender* found that companies headed by high-EQ leadership teams outperform their peers in key areas such as employee retention, customer satisfaction, and financial performance.[14] In an era when workplace burnout and disengagement are major concerns, leaders who can motivate, connect, and create a culture of psychological safety give companies a serious competitive advantage.

Parenthood and the Future of
Leadership Pipelines

If parenthood makes people better leaders, then companies should actively work to retain and promote working parents, yet many fail to do so. A National Bureau of Economic Research study found that nearly one in three women leaves the workforce entirely after having a child, due primarily to unsupportive workplace policies.[15] The cost of this brain drain is staggering. These are not just employees walking out the door—they are future executives, mentors, and decision makers whose potential is lost.

But some companies have recognized this and are taking action. After implementing equal paid parental leave for all employees, Ernst & Young (EY)[16] saw a dramatic drop in female turnover and reduced the gender turnover gap from 15 percent to nearly zero, highlighting how strong parental support policies can improve midcareer retention and promote gender equity in leadership. Google extended paid parental leave from twelve to eighteen weeks after discovering that mothers who took shorter leaves were twice as likely to leave the company. Unilever has implemented leadership training programs specifically designed for employees returning from parental leave, leading to higher engagement and career growth among working parents.

The numbers paint a clear picture. Companies that support working parents don't just retain talent—they develop stronger leaders. Organizations that fail to do so will continue to lose some of their best and brightest to competitors who understand that parenthood is not an obstacle to leadership—it is one of the best training grounds for it.

For years, businesses have operated under the flawed assumption that parenthood makes employees less committed, less focused, and less valuable to the workplace. But the reality is the opposite. Parenthood cultivates the very skills that define exceptional leadership—resilience, decision making, emotional intelligence, and the ability to manage high-pressure situations.

Companies that recognize this will have stronger, more capable leaders who are prepared for the complex challenges of today's business world. Those that don't will continue to suffer from high attrition, weak leadership pipelines, and lost institutional knowledge.

The evidence is clear: if businesses are serious about developing the best leaders, they should start by supporting their employees who are parents.

In the following section, we'll explore another overlooked advantage of embracing working parents—their role in building a more diverse, equitable, and inclusive workforce.

Inclusion and Its Business Benefits

A growing Silicon Valley tech company faced a persistent problem. Despite aggressive recruitment efforts aimed at improving diversity, women and employees from underrepresented backgrounds were leaving at an alarming rate. Leadership conducted exit interviews, expecting to hear the usual complaints—lack of mentorship, an exclusionary culture, limited advancement opportunities, and the like. Instead, they uncovered a far simpler but more damning truth: the company had made it nearly impossible to be both a parent and an employee.

There was no paid parental leave beyond the legal minimum, no accommodations for parents returning from leave, and no flexible work policies that would allow caregivers to balance their professional and family responsibilities. As a result, midcareer professionals—many of them women—were leaving not because they wanted to, but because they had little choice.

This company is not alone. The corporate world has spent decades promoting diversity, equity, and inclusion initiatives, investing billions in unconscious bias training, mentorship programs, and equitable hiring practices. Yet many businesses still fail to recognize that one of the most significant diversity issues in the workplace is parenthood itself. When companies fail to support working parents, they sabotage their own DEI efforts.

Parenthood as a Diversity and Inclusion Issue

The penalties associated with parenthood are not distributed evenly. Studies show that when men become fathers, they are often rewarded—seen as more stable, more committed, and even more deserving of promotions. Women, however, experience the opposite. A study published in the *American Sociological Review* found that a woman's earnings drop by an average of 4 percent for every child she has, while men's earnings increase by 6 percent when they become fathers.[17] The assumption that women will be less committed to their jobs after having children continues to pervade workplace cultures, despite overwhelming evidence that working mothers are often more efficient and productive than their childless peers.

The hiring process itself is riddled with biases against parents. In a now-famous experiment, Correll et al sent out two sets of identical résumés—one that included subtle indicators of parenthood (such as volunteer experience with a parent–teacher association) and one that did not. The results were striking: mothers were 79 percent less likely to be hired and were offered significantly lower salaries than equally qualified women who were not parents. Fathers, by contrast, faced no such penalty and were sometimes even favored over non-fathers.

For women of color, the challenges are even greater. A report by Lean In and McKinsey & Company found that Black mothers are twice as likely as White mothers to be their family's primary breadwinner yet are given fewer workplace accommodations and less flexibility.[18] When companies fail to support working parents, they are not just losing employees, they are disproportionately losing women and people of color, weakening their leadership pipeline and deepening existing inequities.

The Business Impact of Overlooking Parent-Inclusive Policies

The cost of ignoring these racial and socioeconomic disparities is has a morall and financial impact. Companies that fail to retain diverse talent suffer significant economic consequences. A study by McKinsey & Company found that organizations with diverse leadership teams outperform their competitors by 36 percent in profitability, largely because diverse teams make better decisions, drive greater innovation, and attract top-tier talent.[19]

The Swedish company Spotify provides a compelling example of what happens when businesses take a more generous approach. In 2015, the company implemented six months of fully paid parental leave for all employees, regardless of gender, location, or level within the company. The policy was met with skepticism—some executives worried about the cost, while others feared a drop in productivity. Instead, the results were overwhelmingly positive. Employee retention soared, especially among women, and applications for open positions increased by 20 percent, attracting top talent eager to work for a company that valued work–life balance. Perhaps most notably, female leadership representation grew significantly, as more women were able to continue their careers without being forced out by rigid workplace structures.

Spotify's success is not an anomaly. The Boston Consulting Group found that companies with strong parental leave and flexible work policies consistently have higher female representation in leadership roles, which in turn leads to better financial performance. A Stanford University study found that hybrid work arrangements have no negative impact on productivity and significantly improve employee retention—underscoring that supporting working parents through flexible policies isn't just a social good, but a clear business advantage.[20]

Changing Expectations of the Workforce

Support for working parents is becoming even more urgent as the workforce itself changes. The workforce is increasingly made up of millennials and Gen Z, two large generational cohorts that will dominate the new parents in the workplace over the next two decades. Their views of inclusion, work–life balance, and families/family roles will define what employers need to do to compete for talent.

Millennials, now the largest generation in the labor market, are also the most likely to be parents of young children. For Gen Z, the youngest segment of the workforce, flexibility and work–life balance are even more critical. For the first time in the twenty-two-year history of Randstad's global workforce survey, work–life balance was ranked the top priority by employees—named by 83 percent of Gen Z respondents—surpassing both job security and pay as the most important factor in choosing or staying in a job.[21] This finding suggests that companies without strong parental support policies will struggle to attract and retain the next generation of talent.

Some of the most successful companies have already adapted to this shift. Netflix offers paid parental leave for the first year after a child's birth, a policy that has helped the company maintain one of the lowest turnover rates in the entertainment industry. When Accenture extended its paid maternity leave from eight to sixteen weeks, they experienced an impressive 40 percent reduction in attrition among new mothers, underscoring how enhanced parental support policies can significantly boost retention.[22] Salesforce implemented a parental mentorship program to help employees transition back to work, resulting in stronger engagement and leadership development.

The Cost of Inaction

Despite successes logged by Netflix, Google, Accenture, Salesforce, and other forward-thinking organizations, many companies still fail to take action, clinging to outdated workplace models that do not reflect the realities of modern parenthood. The risks of inaction are significant. Companies that fail to support working parents face higher turnover rates, increased recruitment costs, and lower overall employee engagement. In an era of unprecedented workplace transparency, businesses that neglect these issues also risk serious reputational damage. Employees today have platforms—Glassdoor, LinkedIn, social media—where they can publicly call out companies for failing to support working parents.

In the long run, these organizations will find themselves at a competitive disadvantage, losing top talent to employers that recognize the undeniable link between parenthood and workplace equity.

For decades, businesses have operated under the assumption that diversity, equity, and inclusion efforts are separate from parental support initiatives. But the evidence is clear: parenthood is a DEI issue, and companies that ignore it are undermining their own diversity and inclusion goals. Organizations that prioritize working parents through robust parental leave, flexible work arrangements, and career development programs don't just foster more inclusive workplaces, they attract and retain top talent, improve financial performance, and future-proof their workforce.

The companies that embrace this reality will gain a competitive edge. Those that don't will continue to lose their best people—to burnout, to competitors, and to industries that recognize what has been true all along: supporting parents is not just good for employees, it's smart business.

The Cost of NOT Supporting Parents

A senior manager at a Fortune 500 company returned from maternity leave eager to reengage with her team and pick up where she left off. She had spent years climbing the corporate ladder, consistently outperforming expectations. But on her first day back, she noticed something had shifted. Projects she had previously led had been reassigned. Conversations about promotions, once frequent, had disappeared. Meetings were scheduled at odd hours, making daycare pickups impossible.

Over the next few months, she watched as her opportunities dwindled. Her performance was no different than before—if anything, she was more efficient, more focused, more capable—but her manager's and colleagues' perception of her had changed. The unspoken assumption was that she was now less committed, less ambitious, less valuable. Frustrated, she eventually left for a competitor that offered flexible work arrangements and a leadership track for returning parents.

This manager's story is not unique. It plays out in companies across industries, with businesses quietly hemorrhaging some of their most talented employees because they fail to recognize the realities of working parents. And the cost? It's astronomical—not only for individuals but for companies themselves.

The High Cost of Attrition

Every year, businesses spend billions of dollars replacing employees they could have retained with better policies. As described earlier in this chapter, the cost of attrition is shockingly high. Parents, especially mothers, are among the most frequent victims of workplace attrition. According to AARP and the National Alliance for Caregiving, 39 percent of caregivers have left a job to have more time for caregiving, with 34 percent reporting they quit because their jobs lacked flexible hours; many never return to their previous career trajectory.[23] And yet, most of these departures could have been avoided. When companies provide robust family leave policies, including paid leave, workplace flexibility, and structured reentry support, women who take leave are up to 93 percent more likely to remain employed nine to twelves months after childbirth, according to the Boston Consulting Group.[24]

Contrast that with companies that ignore these realities. Recall the SHRM study we cited earlier: businesses that fail to provide meaningful parental support face 25 to 30 percent higher turnover rates among employees with children. The departure of just a handful of high-performing employees each year—especially those with specialized knowledge or leadership potential—can weaken an organization's competitive edge and institutional memory.

Burnout and Declining Productivity

Even for parents who remain in the workforce, the absence of adequate support takes a toll—on engagement, mental health, and productivity. A 2022 study conducted by the Ohio State University found that 66 percent of working parents reported experiencing burnout, due largely to the impossibility of juggling work and caregiving responsibilities.[25] When employees are stretched too thin, productivity plummets, absenteeism rises, and innovation suffers.

The irony is that many companies assume they are saving money by resisting parental benefits when, in reality, they are paying the price through lower efficiency and disengaged employees. This was precisely the issue at a major investment firm in New York, where internal surveys revealed that many high-potential employees—particularly women—were struggling to balance work and family life. Instead of implementing changes, leadership doubled down on rigid office policies. Within two years, half of the firm's female midlevel managers had left, taking their skills and institutional knowledge with them.

Reputational Damage and the War for Talent

The job market has changed. As we described earlier, younger generations of employees expect more from their employers, not just in terms of salary, but also in values and workplace culture. Companies that fail to recognize this shift risk serious reputational damage and struggle to attract top talent.

In extreme cases, failing to support working parents can even lead to legal risks and public backlash. A major tech firm was sued by employees who alleged that new mothers were systematically pushed out of leadership tracks. The lawsuit damaged the firm's reputation and forced leadership to overhaul its parental leave and flexibility policies.

Companies that assume they can ignore these trends are making a costly miscalculation. The war for talent is fierce, and organizations that fail to create parent-inclusive workplaces will struggle to attract and retain the best employees, ultimately weakening their competitive position.

Actionable Strategies for Companies

An executive at a global financial firm made a radical proposal. The firm was losing female employees at twice the rate of its male employees, and exit interviews revealed a common thread—new parents felt unsupported and overwhelmed. The executive suggested a solution: extend paid parental leave, implement a structured return-to-work program, and introduce flexible scheduling options.

The pushback was immediate. Skeptics within the company warned that costs would skyrocket, clients would be frustrated, and the culture of high performance would suffer. But with retention numbers dwindling, leadership agreed to a trial program. Within a year, the results were undeniable. Attrition among new parents dropped by 40 percent, productivity among returning employees increased, and company morale improved so dramatically that even nonparents reported feeling more engaged. The program was eventually expanded worldwide, and today, the firm is one of the most sought-after employers in its industry.

This case study highlights a critical truth: supporting working parents is not just about implementing policies—it's about embedding parent-inclusive strategies into a company's culture. When businesses make deliberate changes, they see measurable benefits in retention, productivity, and leadership development. But what exactly should companies do? We speak to specific actions throughout the following chapters.

Conclusion: The Path Forward

For decades, businesses have operated under a flawed assumption: that employees who become parents are less committed, less available, and less valuable. This assumption has shaped policies, hiring practices, and corporate culture, often to the detriment of working parents, particularly women. But as we've seen, the data tells a different story.

Working parents are some of the most productive, efficient, and emotionally intelligent employees in the workforce. They develop leadership skills, crisis management abilities, and prioritization techniques that make them assets to any organization. Companies that recognize this and invest in parent-inclusive policies see higher retention, better performance, and a stronger leadership pipeline. Those that don't face higher turnover, lower engagement, and long-term damage to their brand and bottom line.

The companies that win in the future will be the ones that evolve now. They will be the ones that see parenthood not as a burden but as an incubator for some of the strongest talent available. They will implement meaningful policies—not just because it's the right thing to do, but because it's the smartest business decision they can make.

So, where does this leave us? The path forward is clear. The workplace is changing, and the companies that adapt will thrive. The question is no longer whether businesses should support working parents, the question is whether they can afford not to.

It's time to rethink the way we see parenthood in the workplace: not as a roadblock, not as a liability, but as one of the greatest untapped resources for business success.

Key Takeaways

- **Parenthood builds stronger leaders.** Parents develop critical leadership skills like resilience, crisis management, and emotional intelligence, making them invaluable employees.
- **Ignoring parents is costly.** Companies that fail to support working parents face higher turnover, lower engagement, and lost talent.
- **Parental support is an inclusion issue.** Without strong policies, businesses risk widening gender and racial inequalities in leadership.
- **Flexibility and leave improve retention.** Paid leave, flexible work, and structured return programs drive loyalty and productivity.
- **Companies that support parents win.** Businesses that embrace working parents attract top talent and build stronger leadership pipelines.

Reflection

1. How does losing parent employees impact your company's leadership and diversity?
2. What are the biggest risks your business faces by failing to support parents?
3. If you could implement one policy to help working parents, what would it be?
4. How will shifting workforce expectations change the way your company supports parents in the future?

3 | PENALTIES AND BONUSES

In the summer of 2018, two employees at the same company walked into their annual performance reviews. The first, a thirty-five-year-old marketing director named Lisa, had just returned from maternity leave. The second, a forty-two-year-old director of sales named Marcus, had recently welcomed his second child. Both had stellar records. Both had exceeded their quarterly targets. But when the reviews came in, their trajectories diverged.

Lisa's feedback was glowing—her manager praised her leadership and creativity—but there was an asterisk. He suggested she take on fewer "high-pressure" projects in the coming year so she could "focus on her family." He assured her this wasn't a demotion, just an adjustment for work–life balance. Her raise? A modest bump, less than the increases her peers received.

Marcus, on the other hand, was framed as a rising star. "Fatherhood has really settled him," one senior executive noted. "He's more dependable than ever." He was assigned to a new high-profile account, and seen as someone ready for the next step. His raise? Substantial.

Neither Lisa nor Marcus had asked for any of this. Lisa hadn't requested fewer responsibilities. Marcus hadn't petitioned for a promotion. But unwritten rules were shaping their careers. Lisa was experiencing the *motherhood penalty*, a well-documented workplace bias where women with children are perceived as less committed, less ambitious, and—ironically—less deserving of leadership opportunities. Marcus, meanwhile, was benefiting from the *fatherhood bonus*, an invisible boost that rewards men for having children by viewing them as more stable, dedicated, and career oriented.

Bias isn't always a conscious decision. It operates in the background, influencing decisions in ways that feel natural to those making them. Managers aren't necessarily trying to hold women back or push men forward—they're acting on deeply ingrained societal scripts about work, gender, and family. These biases aren't limited to parents either; they shape the careers of child-free employees, nontraditional caregivers, and anyone who doesn't fit the assumed mold of the "ideal worker."

And yet, biases aren't uniformly negative. While some groups face barriers, others are granted unearned advantages. The motherhood penalty exists alongside the fatherhood bonus. The assumption that mothers are distracted at work parallels the assumption that single, child-free employees are always available. Biases penalize some, reward others, and leave a lasting impact on workplace dynamics.

The question, then, is not just how to overcome these biases, but how to make them visible in the first place. What happens when we stop seeing these patterns as individual quirks and start recognizing them as structural forces? What if we could reshape our workplaces so that success wasn't determined by whether or not you have children, but by your actual contributions?

Understanding Workplace Biases

On a Monday morning, two hiring managers sat across from each other in a conference room, reviewing a stack of résumés. They were looking for a new senior analyst—someone sharp, strategic, and ready to lead projects. After flipping through a few applications, one of the managers paused.

"She looks great," he said, pointing to a candidate with an impressive background in finance. "But she just had a baby, right? Do you think she'll be able to handle the travel requirements?"

His colleague nodded thoughtfully. "Good point. Let's flag that. We need someone fully committed."

Five minutes later, they reviewed another candidate. "This guy's solid," one of them remarked. "And he just became a dad! He will probably be even more motivated now to get out of the house."

Neither of them realized what had just happened. In the span of a few minutes, they had upheld one of the most persistent workplace biases without even knowing it. The woman was penalized for her parenthood; the man was rewarded for his.

This is how bias works—not in the form of explicit discrimination, but in the quiet, casual moments of decision making.

Implicit vs. Explicit Bias

Explicit bias is easy to spot. It's the manager who says, "We don't hire women because they'll just leave to have kids" or the executive who refuses to promote anyone working part-time. But these overt forms of discrimination are increasingly rare—partly because they're illegal and partly because they conflict with modern workplace values.

Implicit bias, however, is far more elusive. It's the recruiter who unconsciously assumes that child-free employees are "hungrier" for promotions. It's the colleague who expects a new mom to skip the business trip but assumes a new dad will still go. It's the hiring manager who doesn't even realize why one résumé feels more "right" than another.

The Harvard Implicit Association Test (IAT), one of the most widely used tools for measuring unconscious bias, has shown again and again that people—even those who believe in gender equality—associate men with careers and women with family. These mental shortcuts are often shaped by decades of cultural conditioning and influence everything from hiring decisions to performance evaluations.

Gender is an important insider–outsider dynamic and it intersects powerfully with parental status.

Insider–Outsider Dynamics:
The Power Structures Behind Workplace Bias

Biases related to parental status do not exist in a vacuum; they are reinforced by broader power structures within the workplace. These power structures create what we call *insider–outsider dynamics*—unspoken rules that determine who has the advantage in a given environment and who must adjust to fit in.

Understanding these dynamics is key to recognizing why working parents often face career penalties, why fathers receive a professional boost, and why employees without children are sometimes expected to take on extra work without additional recognition.

What Are Insider–Outsider Dynamics?

In any social system, there are insiders—those for whom the environment is designed—and outsiders—those who must adjust to succeed. These dynamics are present in nearly every aspect of identity, from race and gender to socioeconomic status and ableness. The workplace is no exception.

A useful analogy is handedness. Right-handed people rarely think about their dominant hand because the world is designed for them—scissors, desks, keyboards, and even the direction of writing assume dexterity with the right hand. Left-handed people, on the other hand, are constantly aware of their handedness because they must adjust to tools and systems that weren't designed for them. The same is true in workplace culture: those who fit the mold of the "ideal worker" rarely notice the structures that benefit them, while those who deviate from the norm must overcome often subtle barriers and make constant adjustments.

The Workplace as a Nonparent-Centric System

Historically, workplaces were designed for a workforce that was largely male, single income, and unencumbered by caregiving responsibilities. While policies have evolved, the *ideal worker norm* remains deeply embedded in organizational culture. The expectation is still that the most dedicated employees are those who are always available, unburdened by external responsibilities, and willing to prioritize work above all else.

In this framework, nonparents are often the workplace insiders, while parents are outsiders—at least in the transition phase of becoming a parent. Nonparents generally don't have to think about their identity as nonparents; they operate in a system that assumes their full availability. Many parents, however, must navigate biases that assume their career ambitions have diminished or that their productivity will suffer.

This dynamic is particularly evident in the way managers make assumptions about working parents. When a mother-to-be announces her pregnancy, she often encounters concerns about her future availability, even if she has demonstrated unwavering commitment to her career. Fathers, on the other hand, may be seen as more responsible and dependable after having children. These biases do not arise from explicit discrimination but rather from subconscious expectations about who belongs in leadership roles and who does not.

The Complications of Insider–Outsider Status

Unlike some characteristics—race, for example—parental status is a fluid identity. Everyone starts as a nonparent, and many transition into parenthood. This creates an interesting tension: those who were once insiders may suddenly find themselves navigating outsider status, adjusting to a workplace that was not necessarily designed for them.

Moreover, insider–outsider dynamics related to parenthood are complicated by other intersecting identities. Gender plays a significant role—as we've discussed, mothers often experience penalties, while fathers may experience bonuses. Socioeconomic status, marital status, and cultural background also shape how parental identity is perceived in the workplace. A single mother without financial support may be seen differently than a father in a dual-income household, even though both are parents.

The Cycle of Bias Reinforcement

The insider–outsider dynamic feeds a self-perpetuating cycle. When organizations assume that parents, particularly mothers, will be less committed, they are less likely to offer them career-advancing opportunities. Over time, this lack of opportunities leads to fewer parents in leadership, reinforcing the perception that parenthood and professional ambition are at odds.

Similarly, when child-free employees are routinely expected to take on extra work, they may begin to feel resentment, reinforcing an "us vs. them" mentality between parents and nonparents. This division prevents organizations from creating a truly inclusive and equitable work environment where all employees, regardless of parental status, feel valued and supported.

Challenging the Insider–Outsider Norm

Recognizing and challenging these dynamics is essential for fostering a workplace culture that values contributions over outdated assumptions. Organizations must actively dismantle the biases that reinforce insider–outsider hierarchies, ensuring that success is determined not by whether someone has children but by the actual impact they bring to their work.

By integrating a more nuanced understanding of these dynamics into talent management, performance evaluations, and flexibility policies, companies can move beyond the penalties and bonuses of parenthood and toward a more equitable workplace for all. Now let's explore some common types of bias in the workplace and how they impact specific group memberships.

Confirmation Bias: Seeing What We Expect

Imagine you've just hired a new employee. You've been told she's a mother of two. Over the next few months, you notice that she occasionally leaves work early for school events. Her emails sometimes come late at night, after her kids are in bed. Without even realizing it, your brain starts making connections: *She's distracted. She's not as invested in work. She has other priorities.*

Now, imagine you've hired another employee. You know he doesn't have kids. Over the next few months, you notice that he stays late at the office. He sends emails on weekends. Again, your brain makes a connection: *He's dedicated. He's serious about his career. He's committed.* However, you do not know how he is using his time. Is he doing work? Is he staying late because he is meeting someone for dinner nearby or spending time on his social media? Any conclusions are based on appearance and assumptions.

This is confirmation bias—our tendency to notice and remember information that supports our preexisting beliefs while ignoring data that contradicts them. In a workplace setting, it means that managers, often without realizing it, reinforce stereotypes rather than evaluating performance objectively.

Many studies have found that confirmation bias is particularly strong in high-stakes professional settings. Managers tend to unconsciously seek out evidence that aligns with their initial perceptions of employees, leading to self-fulfilling prophecies. If a manager believes working parents are less committed, they will notice the moments that confirm this assumption and overlook the moments that disprove it.

Affinity Bias: The "Like Me" Effect

A software company analyzed its hiring patterns and made an unsettling discovery. Nearly 90 percent of its leadership team had one thing in common: they were men without children. No one had intentionally created this dynamic. The company prided itself on being progressive. But when they looked at the data, the pattern was undeniable.

Affinity bias—our natural preference for people who resemble us—is one of the most powerful and least discussed workplace biases. It's why hiring managers often choose candidates who "feel like a good fit." It's why leaders tend to mentor employees who remind them of themselves at an earlier stage in their careers. And it's why so many industries end up with homogenous leadership teams, even when their hiring policies appear neutral.

For parents, affinity bias can be a double-edged sword. A manager who is also a working parent might be more empathetic to a direct report balancing childcare and work. But if leadership is dominated by employees without caregiving responsibilities, parents may be quietly shut out of key opportunities—not because of open discrimination but because decision makers unconsciously favor those who share their lifestyle.

A 2009 study published in the *Journal of Labor Economics* found that managers are more likely to hire employees who share demographic similarities—highlighting how these similarities can influence hiring decisions.[1] This means that as long as workplaces are led by individuals with fewer caregiving responsibilities, those without these responsibilities will continue to be overrepresented in leadership.

The Invisible Structures Shaping Success

The biases we are describing, the penalties and bonuses, are often both unconscious and unintentional. They become automatic and get built into the system. When people think about workplace bias, they often imagine overt discrimination. But in reality, bias operates more like a set of hidden rules—unspoken advantages for some, unspoken barriers for others. Most companies wouldn't intend to create these sorts of disparities because they aren't productive. There are many well-intentioned companies, but any company that wants to be effective doesn't rest on its intent; it gets busy aligning its intentions with the actual impact of its policies and actions.

What if we stopped viewing success in the workplace as purely meritocratic and started recognizing these invisible forces? What if organizations actively sought to identify and dismantle these biases instead of letting them shape career trajectories? Because here's the thing: bias isn't just about fairness—it's about effectiveness. Companies that fail to acknowledge these dynamics lose out on talent. They overlook skilled employees. They limit innovation by fostering homogeneity.

In the next section, we'll explore how these biases don't just shape individual careers, they structure entire industries, creating penalties for some and bonuses for others in ways that ultimately impact everyone.

The Motherhood Penalty

Before we dive deeper into the motherhood penalty, let's take a moment to recognize that being a woman in the workplace has been and continues to be challenging for women regardless of their parental status. As we go into Erin's story, realize that motherhood is layered on top of any existing biases that may be at play. On the day Erin returned from maternity leave, she walked into her office feeling cautiously optimistic. Before she left, she had been leading one of her company's most high-profile product launches. The last email she had received from her manager before giving birth had been filled with praise for her leadership. But as she sat down at her desk, she noticed something strange—her inbox was quiet. No urgent messages. No major project updates. Then she opened her calendar and saw the real shift: her biggest projects, some of which she had been working on for more than a year, had been reassigned—and not just temporarily to cover her leave. No one had told her. No one had consulted her. It was simply assumed that she wouldn't want them back.

Erin's experience is not unique. Women returning from maternity leave often find that their roles have been subtly restructured in their absence. Even when their performance remains strong, career momentum stalls. Sometimes this happens through outright exclusion—being overlooked for promotions or major assignments. Other times, it happens under the guise of "helpfulness"—a manager assumes that reducing a mother's workload is a kindness when, in reality, it's a career setback.

One of the most common manifestations of the penalty is opportunity hoarding—where high-stakes projects, leadership training, or promotions are steered away from mothers in favor of colleagues without children. This often happens with good intentions. A manager might say, "I didn't assign this project to you because I know you have a lot going on with your family." Another term for this action is sidelining. In reality, this "kindness" means fewer leadership opportunities and slower career growth.

The Subtle Cost of Sidelining

One of the most damaging yet often overlooked challenges new parents—especially mothers—face upon returning from leave is being quietly sidelined. This doesn't always take the form of overt discrimination. Instead, it might show up as being passed over for a major project, excluded from strategic conversations, or reassigned to less visible work under the guise of "easing back in."

The type of sidelining women experience is often subtle. The company's policies are progressive and the stated support from managers is clear, but the subtle behaviors and their cumulative impact are dispiriting and have a negative impact on career development, motivation, and retention. For example, one of our interviewees in a very progressive midsize company was assured that her pregnancy and leave would have no negative impact on her career path, that colleagues would "have her back," and that the level and impact of her job wouldn't change. This promise was reassuring and motivating, as before her pregnancy her influence and impact at her company had been growing.

She worked hard right up to the birth of her first child. As the end of her planned leave neared, she noted some changes, which became more apparent when she extended her leave due to family challenges. During her extended leave she was contacted by recruiters, who suggested that this was a good time to make a job change, but she trusted her organization and her colleagues. Upon her return, however, she found her role clearly diminished, though the changes weren't positioned that way. In her first few weeks back in the office, her shrinking role and level of influence became increasingly apparent, leaving her questioning both her decision-making process and her career prospects.

While often well-intentioned, a company's decision to moderate a new parent's role can reinforce the false perception that they are less capable or less committed. In reality, most are eager to reengage and contribute meaningfully—but on terms that acknowledge their recent transition.

Sidelining not only diminishes an employee's growth opportunities, it also erodes their sense of belonging and value. Over time, this subtle marginalization can lead to disengagement and, eventually, a quiet exit from the company. The better alternative? Let the employee lead the conversation about capacity, and assume capability unless they indicate otherwise. Support doesn't mean stepping aside—it means being seen.

Women also face shifts in their managers' perceptions about their performance. Before having children, a woman may be viewed as highly ambitious, focused, and leadership-ready. After becoming a mother, those same qualities are often questioned. A 2007 study published in the *American Journal of Sociology* found that mothers were rated as less competent, less committed, and less promotable than equally qualified women without children, despite having similar qualifications and experience.[2] The assumption? That their attention was now divided, even if there was no evidence to support that view.

Meanwhile, the motherhood penalty extends to financial compensation as well. Unlike others who interrupt their careers—to take time off for graduate school or a sabbatical, for example—mothers do not see their wages rebound in subsequent years. Instead, the earnings gap compounds, contributing directly to the lack of female representation in leadership roles.

Why Flexibility Isn't a Solution but a Trap

When women encounter career obstacles after having children, they are often advised to seek out more flexible work arrangements. On the surface, this seems like a reasonable solution—after all, flexibility allows for better work–life balance. We even encourage it, especially in the first few months of returning from leave, in a later chapter of this book. But in many workplaces, flexibility comes at a hidden cost:

- Mothers who work remotely or part-time are promoted less frequently; while fathers who work part time or from home are also less likely to be promoted, there are far fewer men who adjust their schedules after having a child.
- Women who request flexibility are often assigned to lower-visibility projects.
- In performance evaluations, flexibility is often conflated with a lack of ambition.

While flexible work policies are widely sought by women, a striking 95 percent believe that using them will negatively impact their career progression, according to Deloitte's *Women @ Work* report.[3] This viewpoint isn't because women think they are less capable—it's because managers often associate flexibility with decreased career ambition.

Erin, for example, decided to work remotely two days a week after her maternity leave. Within six months, she noticed that major client accounts were being assigned to colleagues who were in the office full-time. Her performance reviews remained strong, but the fast-track career path she had been on before motherhood had vanished.

This phenomenon, known as the flexibility stigma, is a key driver of the motherhood penalty. It punishes women for using the very policies that are supposed to help them stay in the workforce.

The Long-Term Career Consequences
of the Motherhood Penalty

Perhaps the most damaging aspect of the motherhood penalty is that it is not temporary. Many women assume that once their children reach school age, their careers will rebound. But research suggests the opposite: the career setbacks women experience in their thirties due to motherhood ripple through their entire careers.

The 2022 *Women in the Workplace* report from McKinsey & Company and LeanIn.org found that women leaders—particularly mothers—are far more likely than their male peers to report that being a parent has played a role in being passed over for promotions they were qualified for.[4] This contributes to the leadership gap, where women hold only 10 percent of Fortune 500 CEO positions, despite making up nearly half the workforce.

The motherhood penalty also influences retention. Women who feel stalled in their careers are more likely to leave their companies, either to start their own businesses or to seek environments that better support their ambitions. This, in turn, leads to fewer women in leadership, reinforcing the cycle.

Breaking the Cycle: What Companies Can Do

While the motherhood penalty is deeply ingrained, it is not inevitable. Companies that are serious about retaining and advancing women must take intentional steps to challenge the assumptions that fuel it.

First, managers must stop making decisions on behalf of mothers. Instead of assuming that a mother wants a lighter workload or fewer responsibilities, the manager must ask her directly. Some may want a slower pace—but many do not. Communication is key here. These conversations do not come naturally, so corporations need to provide training for their managers if they want to truly impact the culture.

Second, performance evaluations must focus on actual results, not assumptions about availability or commitment. By using objective performance metrics, rather than subjective impressions of "engagement," companies can ensure that mothers are judged by the same standards as their peers.

Finally, organizations need to redesign flexibility policies so that they benefit all employees—parents and nonparents alike. When flexibility becomes the norm rather than a special accommodation, its career penalties disappear.

The motherhood penalty persists not because women become less ambitious after having children, but because workplaces continue to operate under outdated assumptions and fail to challenge them directly. The real challenge is not balancing work and family—it is changing the way work itself is structured. Until companies recognize and dismantle these biases, they will continue to push talented women out of leadership—and lose some of their most capable employees in the process.

The Fatherhood Bonus

A management consulting firm analyzed internal promotion rates in an effort to understand patterns in career advancement. What they found was unsurprising but revealing: women who became mothers were promoted at lower rates than their child-free female peers, consistent with the well-documented motherhood penalty. But a second, less-discussed pattern also emerged—men who became fathers were promoted at significantly higher rates than men without children. The same life event—parenthood—was holding back one group while propelling another forward.

This phenomenon, often called the fatherhood bonus, is the mirror image of the motherhood penalty. A *New York Times* article echoed our earlier mention that after having children, men's earnings increased by an average of 6 percent, while women's earnings declined by 4 percent per child.[5] Separate research found that fathers were perceived as more stable, dependable, and leadership-ready, while mothers were seen as less committed, less available, and more likely to put family before career.

Why Fathers Are Rewarded for Parenthood

The pattern of rewarding men for fatherhood plays out in subtle but measurable ways. Take David, a marketing director at a tech firm. Before becoming a father, he was a strong but unremarkable performer, seen as competent and reliable but not necessarily as an up-and-coming leader. After his wife gave birth to their first child, however, his career trajectory changed. His manager began assigning him more leadership-heavy projects, citing his "newfound focus and long-term investment in the company's future." At his next review, David was praised for his maturity and increased sense of responsibility—qualities his employer tied directly to fatherhood. As we will discuss later in the book, parents do acquire skills that relate directly to work, so this would not be out of line, except that his wife, Ana, experienced the motherhood penalty at the exact same time in the same organization.

David's case is not unusual. A 2021 study published in the *International Journal of Organizational Leadership* found that fatherhood is associated with measurable improvements in leadership behaviors, suggesting that men with children may be perceived as more capable leaders, potentially contributing to their being fast-tracked for promotion.[6] This bias is particularly strong in industries that emphasize long-term client relationships, financial stability, and leadership potential, areas where fatherhood is seen as reinforcing rather than disrupting professional ambition.

This pattern also explains why single, child-free men often do not receive the same career benefits as their fatherhood-track peers even when there may be a perception that the ideal leader is a man without outside responsibilities. In the same way that women without children tend to advance faster than mothers, men without children tend to advance more slowly than fathers. This discrepancy is not because fathers become better employees overnight—it's because cultural narratives position fatherhood as a sign of "settling down" and becoming more serious about work.

The Double Standard in Work–Life Balance Perceptions

One of the clearest indicators of the fatherhood bonus is the way flexible work arrangements are perceived differently for men and women. When a mother requests a modified schedule or remote workday, she risks being labeled as someone whose priorities have shifted away from her job. When a father makes the same request, it is more likely to be framed as an admirable attempt to "be there for his kids" while still being dedicated to his career.

Sociologist Michelle Budig has studied the dynamic around work–life balance extensively. Her research found that fathers who requested flexibility were praised for being family oriented and committed to work–life balance, while mothers making identical requests were perceived as lacking ambition or being unable to manage their responsibilities effectively. These stereotypes don't just affect individual careers—they shape entire workplace cultures, reinforcing the outdated notion that caregiving is a woman's duty while work remains a man's priority.

This cultural perception gap means that men who take parental leave or openly embrace caregiving responsibilities still face challenges, but they often avoid the long-term career penalties that women encounter. A 2013 study published in the *Journal of Social Issues* found that men who requested family leave were perceived as less committed and competent, facing a stigma typically associated with femininity and weakness.[7] However, these penalties tended to be more situational and reversible. In contrast, women who took maternity leave were more likely to experience a lasting decline in perceived commitment and were less likely to be promoted in the two years following their leave.

The Career Trade-Offs for Fathers Who Buck the Trend

Although the fatherhood bonus exists, it does not benefit all fathers equally. The traditional fatherhood bonus rewards men who conform to workplace expectations of dedication, availability, and ambition, but it can work against those who actively challenge these norms.

For fathers who want to be primary caregivers or take a more hands-on role in family life, the benefits of fatherhood disappear—and in some cases, these men experience the same penalties that mothers do. Carlos, a senior consultant, experienced this phenomenon firsthand when he requested a flexible schedule to accommodate his newborn's childcare needs. "My boss was supportive in theory," he recalled. "But there was this lingering assumption that my wife should be the one adjusting her schedule. The moment I asked for something outside the usual career trajectory, it felt like I was breaking some unspoken rule." Carlos described the anxiety he felt when he asked for the full amount of parental leave. "The policies are supportive, the words are supportive, but I can tell that my boss is surprised and not happy that I am taking the third month of leave that our policy entitles me to."

This double standard pressures fathers to maintain the appearance of full professional commitment while simultaneously reinforcing traditional gender roles that penalize mothers. In other words, the fatherhood bonus exists only as long as men don't challenge the status quo.

Our research confirms that fathers who request parental leave or actively pursue flexible work arrangements face a moderate career penalty—not as severe as the one mothers experience, but enough to deter many men from embracing a more active caregiving role. More than 75 percent of the men we interviewed for this book identified this sort of career penalty, and it concerned them, but most agreed that their women partners faced a steeper challenge.

Rethinking the Parenthood Bonus—For Everyone

The problem isn't that fathers are rewarded for having children—it's that mothers aren't. If workplaces truly evaluated employees based on merit, the same stability, time management, and leadership skills attributed to fatherhood would also be recognized in motherhood. Instead of stripping fathers of their advantages, the solution lies in extending the same opportunities to everyone, regardless of gender or parental status.

One way to do this is by equalizing parental leave policies. Research has shown that when fathers take longer paternity leave, the bias against mothers in the workplace is reduced. Countries like Sweden, which offer gender-neutral parental leave, have seen shifts in employer perceptions of caregiving, resulting in more men taking time off and fewer women experiencing long-term career penalties.

Another approach is to track and correct disparities in promotions, pay raises, and high-profile assignments. If companies find that fathers are advancing at higher rates than other employees, it's worth asking: Are these promotions truly based on performance, or are they the result of unconscious bias?

Finally, managers must rethink the cues that signals commitment and leadership in the workplace. Long hours and constant availability are not the hallmarks of the best employees—strategic thinking, adaptability, and problem solving are. Parenthood, in all its forms, cultivates these very qualities.

Instead of a fatherhood bonus, workplaces should embrace a performance bonus, one that rewards all employees based on merit, not outdated stereotypes about who is more dedicated, responsible, or ambitious.

By recognizing and addressing these biases, organizations can ensure that success is determined not by who someone is but by what they contribute. Biases also impact employees without children, as we will consider in the next section.

Biases That Affect Nonparents

We will now shift focus to another overlooked workplace dynamic: how child-free employees are often expected to pick up the slack, work longer hours, and sacrifice personal time, all because they don't have children.

One Tuesday afternoon, Sarah sat in a team meeting, jotting down notes as her manager discussed an upcoming product launch. As the discussion wrapped up, he glanced around the table and said, "Alright, we'll need someone to fly out to the client site for a week. Sarah, you're flexible, right? You don't have kids, so this should be easy for you."

It wasn't a question. It was an expectation.

Sarah had seen this pattern play out before. Whenever last-minute travel was required, late-night deadlines loomed, or a project demanded extra hours, the unwritten rule surfaced: employees without kids should be the ones to step up. When Covid hit, Sarah was expected to open the office while her colleagues, some of whom lived closer to the office, stayed at home with their children. It also happened on snow days. Sarah often had to adjust her vacation schedule to accommodate school vacation weeks, when colleagues with children had priority. She received no additional recognition or bonus for being the "on-call" employee.

The issue wasn't just work distribution—it was also perception. While working parents were seen as juggling competing responsibilities, Sarah and other child-free employees were viewed as always available, always on call, always expected to do more.

This is the bias against nonparents: an unspoken workplace dynamic that often leaves child-free employees shouldering extra responsibilities, sometimes without recognition or choice.

"Always Available" Expectations

Workplaces, whether or not they acknowledge it, operate on a hidden social contract: employees with children get flexibility and understanding while employees without children get workload. Child-free employees report feeling overburdened at work compared to their colleagues with children. Many said they were expected to:

- Stay late because "parents need to pick up their kids."
- Work on holidays or weekends because "they don't have family obligations."
- Take on extra projects because "they have more time."

Of course, this isn't written into any company policy, but it's deeply ingrained in workplace culture.

For Chris, a financial analyst with no kids, this bias became especially clear during the pandemic. As his company scrambled to accommodate working parents with school-aged children at home, Chris was asked to take on more client accounts.

At first, he was happy to help. But as the months dragged on, the imbalance became clear. "I was working sixty-hour weeks while some of my colleagues were logging off at 3 p.m.," he said. "I get that they had kids at home, but I had a life too. And no one seemed to care. It was expected because I chose not to have children."

Some of the parents we interviewed remembered similar experiences or perceptions before they became parents. Michele said, "I have to admit, I was sometimes skeptical when one of my colleagues would leave early because they had to take their child to a doctor's appointment. But now that person is me, and the doctor's appointment is real!"

The "Career-First" Bias

There's another layer to the workplace dynamic surrounding non-parents: the assumption that employees without kids are more career-driven than their parenting colleagues. In many organizations, parenthood is viewed as a natural limiter on ambition. Managers assume that once someone has children, their primary focus shifts away from career advancement.

Conversely, employees without children—especially single employees—are often assumed to be on an upward trajectory with no distractions. While it is not always formally acknowledged, reputable surveys from organizations such as SHRM and Hertelier indicate that child-free employees are often assumed to be more available for extra work, including high-stakes projects, travel-heavy assignments, and overtime—based on the perception that they have fewer external obligations.[8]

This bias disproportionately affects younger employees, who are often in the early stages of career building and may feel pressure to prove their dedication by overworking. For Jordan, a twenty-nine-year-old consultant, the expectations were clear. "I got a reputation for being the guy who would always say yes," he said. "And that meant when big projects came up, I was the first name on the list. I didn't mind at first, but over time, I realized I was burning out. And the people who had families? They were encouraged to set boundaries. I wasn't."

The Unspoken Resentment

The imbalance of expectations between parents and nonparents leads to something few companies talk about: resentment. A 2022 survey by ResumeLab, reported by SHRM, found that 70 percent of child-free employees said they were given more work, and 63 percent reported being denied time off, indicating that many nonparents feel their work–life balance suffers compared to colleagues with children.[9] And among employees who reported high workplace stress, child-free workers were significantly more likely to cite unfair work distribution as a major factor.

The resentment isn't because child-free employees dislike parents. It's because they see an unspoken double standard. When a mother leaves early for a school event, no one bats an eye. But when a single employee leaves early for a personal hobby, they often hear: "Must be nice to have all that free time." When a father asks for remote-work privileges, he's seen as a great dad. But when a child-free employee asks for the same flexibility, their dedication is questioned. These subtle disparities create a workplace culture where some employees feel their personal lives are valued more than others'. And this isn't just an interpersonal issue—it has long-term consequences for employee engagement and retention.

Intersectional Bias: Age, Marital Status, and Caregiving

The bias against nonparents doesn't affect everyone equally. It intersects with other workplace biases, including:

- **Age bias**—Younger employees without kids are often
  expected to take on extra work, while older employees may
  face different assumptions about their career commitment.
- **Marital status bias**—Single employees, in particular,
  report being expected to work longer hours, since they
  "don't have a family to go home to."
- **Caregiving bias**—Employees caring for aging parents or
  other family members often find themselves overlooked
  for flexibility because they don't fit the "working parent"
  mold.

Take Rachel, a forty-two-year-old employee who has never had
children but now cares for her elderly mother. She has repeatedly
asked for a flexible schedule to accommodate doctors' appointments, but her requests are met with resistance. "My boss doesn't
see it the same way," she says. "If I were leaving work early for a
kid's soccer game, I know he wouldn't question it. But because
it's my mom, it's somehow not the same."

This reflects a larger issue: workplaces tend to accommodate
traditional family structures while overlooking other forms of
caregiving.

Creating an Equitable Workplace for Everyone

Bias against nonparents isn't just unfair—it's counterproduc-
tive. When companies assume that child-free employees have
unlimited capacity for work, they risk employee burnout and
disengagement, resulting in high turnover.

What's needed is a new approach to workplace flexibility
and responsibility sharing, one that doesn't center exclusively
on parents but includes all employees.

Some solutions:

- **Recognizing and redistributing workload fairly**.
  Companies should be transparent about work allocation,
  ensuring that child-free employees aren't routinely
  overburdened.

- **Expanding caregiving policies beyond parenthood.**
  Flexible work arrangements should apply equally to those
  caring for aging parents, sick family members, or even
  personal mental health.
- **Eliminating the assumption of unlimited availability.**
  Nonparents should have the same right to personal time as
  parents, whether that's for a creative pursuit, a fitness goal,
  or simply to rest.
- **Encouraging open conversations about work–life
  balance.** Managers should check in with all employees,
  not just working parents, to ensure that everyone feels
  valued and respected.

Ultimately, everyone is affected, parent and nonparent, when
organizations don't have carefully considered and comprehensive
approaches and policies toward those who become parents. A
well-thought-out parental leave policy would consider the needs
of nonparents and parents to maintain an equitable workplace. In
one of our interviews for this book, Sophie, a lead talent officer,
acknowledged how her perspective changed when she became a
parent. Before that, she was "often resentful of having to pick up
the workload" when colleagues became parents. She described
the automatic assumption that she and others would manage the
heightened responsibility and the lack of planning for the change:
"It wouldn't have taken much to create a more equitable and balanced outcome; it just seemed nobody had really thought about
it." Workplaces thrive when everyone—nonparents, parents, and
other caregivers—feels like their personal lives are respected. The
future of work isn't about prioritizing one group over another.
It's about ensuring that success, opportunity, and balance aren't
dictated by whether or not you have kids, but by who you are
and what you contribute.

Strategies to Mitigate Bias in the Workplace

Bias is rarely the result of deliberate malice. More often, it's an accumulation of small, seemingly inconsequential decisions—who gets a high-profile project, who is encouraged to take on leadership, who is given the benefit of the doubt in a performance review. Because these decisions feel natural to the people making them, bias thrives in environments where no one stops to ask why certain patterns keep repeating.

The problem isn't just that biases exist; it's that they become self-reinforcing. The mother who is passed over for a promotion because her manager assumes she has "too much on her plate" never gets the chance to prove otherwise. The father who receives a raise because he is seen as more responsible moves up faster than his equally qualified child-free peer. The single employee who is expected to take on extra work because they "have more time" eventually becomes the default staffer for late nights and weekend projects, burning out in the process.

Organizations that are serious about correcting these inequities cannot rely on good intentions alone. They must actively dismantle the biases embedded in their cultures by changing the way they measure performance, distribute work, and define success.

One of the most effective ways to do this is by auditing how decisions are made—who is being promoted, who is getting the biggest raises, and who is being assigned the most demanding projects. When companies like Salesforce and Accenture took a hard look at their internal data, they found clear patterns of bias that weren't apparent on the surface. Women, particularly mothers, were being promoted at lower rates than their male counterparts, and fathers were receiving larger pay increases than both men without children and women with children. Rather than dismissing these findings as mere coincidence, these companies adjusted their processes, ensuring that compensation and career advancement were based on objective performance metrics rather than unconscious perceptions of commitment.

Bias is also embedded in the way companies define leadership. Many organizations cling to the idea of the "ideal worker"—someone who is always available, eager to travel, and willing to put in long hours. This outdated model disproportionately disadvantages caregivers, particularly parents and those with responsibilities outside of work, while reinforcing the assumption that employees without children should automatically take on more. A growing body of research, however, has shown that longer hours do not translate to higher productivity. Studies from Stanford University have demonstrated that employees who work beyond fifty hours a week see diminishing returns, with those logging seventy-hour weeks producing little to no additional output compared with those who work fifty-five hours.[10] The most effective leaders are not those who work the longest but those who work the smartest—something parents, caregivers, and employees who have learned to balance multiple responsibilities tend to do particularly well.

For real change to take hold, flexibility cannot be seen as a perk granted to a select few, nor should it come at a hidden cost to those who use it. When flexibility is extended to everyone, rather than being treated as an exception to the rule, workplaces become more equitable. Spotify, for example, has implemented a "Work from Anywhere" policy that allows employees to tailor their schedules to their needs. The result has been higher employee satisfaction and sustained productivity, with no evidence of reduced commitment or effectiveness.

Perhaps the most powerful tool in dismantling workplace bias is collective awareness. The more employees challenge assumptions—asking why certain people are given opportunities while others are overlooked, why some are rewarded for caregiving while others are penalized—the harder it becomes for these biases to remain invisible. In recent years, employee advocacy groups have pushed for more equitable policies, and in many cases, they have succeeded. At Microsoft, employees petitioned for expanded parental leave policies and won. At an advertising firm in New York, child-free employees successfully lobbied for remote-work options that had previously been granted primarily to parents.

Bias is not an inescapable feature of workplace culture, but it will persist for as long as companies allow it to go unchecked. By confronting these assumptions head-on, ensuring that flexibility benefits all employees, and challenging outdated ideas about what commitment and leadership look like, organizations can create workplaces where success is determined by performance, not personal circumstances. The companies that recognize this and act on it will not only retain their best talent but will also build a culture that is truly fair—one where no one is penalized or rewarded simply for the life they lead outside of work.

Conclusion: Toward a Bias-Conscious Workplace

For years, many companies have operated under the assumption that success is a function of individual effort, that those who work the hardest and contribute the most will naturally rise. But time and again, when organizations take a closer look at their data—who is being promoted, who is getting the best opportunities, who is struggling to advance despite strong performance—a different reality emerges. Success is not always determined by ability or output. It can also be shaped by a series of invisible advantages and disadvantages, reinforcing outdated assumptions about who belongs in leadership, who is fully committed to their job, and who deserves a seat at the table.

The companies that understand this will be the ones that thrive. They will attract and retain the best talent, not because they favor one group over another, but because they have built a culture where everyone has the same chance to succeed.

The path forward is not about removing all bias—that is impossible. Instead, it is about recognizing when bias is at play and making conscious choices to correct it. Because in the end, the goal is not to eliminate the complexities of work and life but to create a workplace where those complexities are acknowledged, understood, and valued rather than penalized or rewarded. The goal is a workplace where success is determined not by outdated assumptions but by what truly matters: talent, effort, and the ability to contribute.

Key Takeaways

- **Bias shapes careers in unseen ways.** The motherhood penalty, fatherhood bonus, and extra burdens on child-free employees create inequities that often go unnoticed.
- **Success should be based on performance, not personal life.** Outdated assumptions about commitment and leadership must be challenged.
- **Flexibility should be for everyone.** Work–life balance policies should support all employees, not just parents.
- **Data reveals hidden bias.** Regular audits of promotions, pay, and workload help ensure fairness.
- **Bias-conscious workplaces perform better.** Organizations that focus on equity attract and retain top talent.

Reflection

1. Have you ever observed or experienced workplace bias related to parenthood or caregiving? How did it manifest?
2. How do current workplace norms reinforce outdated ideas about commitment and leadership? What changes would make the biggest impact?
3. If your organization conducted an audit of promotions, salaries, and workload distribution, what patterns do you think would emerge?
4. What strategies can managers implement to ensure that flexibility benefits all employees, not just certain groups?
5. How can individuals challenge bias in real time—whether in hiring, promotions, or daily workplace interactions—without fear of repercussions?

4 | THE PSYCHOLOGICAL SHIFT TO PARENTHOOD

In the years leading up to the arrival of a child, we may imagine parenthood in idyllic terms: a joyful homecoming, the miracle of birth, the smooth integration of a new family member into an already bustling life. For many, this vision includes a seamless balance between work and home life, a perfect harmony where professional success and personal fulfillment coexist without conflict. The expectation—fueled by social media depictions and workplace norms—is that, with the right planning, the transition into parenthood should be relatively straightforward. The truth, however, is far more complex. In the previous chapter, we spoke about insider–outsider dynamics, which create challenges sometimes subtle or unseen. For women in the workplace, there is an overriding cultural stereotype that derails careers and creates feelings of fear or trepidation. In an interview, a senior executive at a financial firm told us she was scared that becoming a mother would impact her career prospects, as she had seen it create barriers for other women. Men are traversing a changing and confusing landscape, with tension between more father-friendly attitudes and policies and deeply held and perhaps less-conscious traditional concepts of men as career-focused breadwinners.

Sooner or later, corporate managers will have employees transitioning into parenthood, facing the identity shifts and challenges discussed in this chapter. Understanding these changes can help them better support and retain their talent while harnessing the strengths that parenthood can bring to the workplace.

Employee/Parent Identity

The moment a baby enters your life, everything changes. It's a psychological shift unlike any other. The mental recalibration required to go from "just me" or "us" to "parent" is profound, but it is only the beginning. The real transformation lies in the delicate dance between your new role as a parent and your ongoing identity as a professional, two facets of your life that, while deeply interconnected, can seem at odds with each other.

As you immerse yourself in the joy of your child's arrival and also navigate the terrain of late-night feedings, unexpected health concerns, and the pressure of reentering the workplace after parental leave, you may begin to question everything you thought you knew about work–life balance. The carefully constructed boundaries between your personal and professional lives, once so distinct, now blur. You may feel torn between the demands of a child who needs your constant attention, love, and support and a job that requires your focus and ambition. The tension between these roles is not only exhausting but can also lead to feelings of inadequacy, guilt, and frustration.

There is more to this story than the conflict between home and work. At its core, this chapter explores the psychological shift that occurs when you become a parent and the profound effect it has on your identity, your sense of self-worth, and your relationship with your job. We pose three questions: (1) How do we reconcile these two parts of our identity, and how can we adjust our expectations to embrace both roles fully? (2) Are we in a zero-sum game where success in one area implies failure in the other? (3) Can the experience of becoming a parent make us better at our jobs, and vice versa?

For some, the answers lie in reimagining the narrative of parenthood and work—not as an either-or scenario but as a dynamic interplay that, when managed with intention and self-compassion, can lead to growth in both realms. This chapter explores the process of emotional preparation for parenthood, explores the delicate balance of work and life, and argues for a shift toward viewing the experience of parenting as an opportunity for personal and professional growth.

We will take a closer look at the psychological and emotional complexities that working parents face, from the first moments of anticipation to the often jarring and emotionally overwhelming reality of the first few months. The stories of real working parents will help us understand the common struggles we all face in this dual journey. Along the way, we'll explore how self-compassion and personal growth are essential tools in navigating the complexities of work and parenthood, and how companies can build better systems of support to help parents thrive in both roles.

Becoming a parent is a transition that is, in many ways, unpredictable. It's a leap into the unknown, where no amount of preparation can completely prepare you for the emotional, physical, and psychological shifts that will follow. But it is also a journey of growth. And in embracing this growth with self-compassion, we can begin to see that the balance between work and family is not a destination but an ongoing, evolving process.

The Dual Identity: Individual and Parent

Ben, a New York based marketing executive with a sharp wit and a penchant for meticulously planned presentations, found himself at a crossroads. He was holding a mug of coffee in one hand and a baby onesie in the other, the telltale signs of a transition he had put off contemplating. For years, Ben's identity was neatly defined. He was a rising star in the firm, the go-to man for last-minute pitches, the guy colleagues described as "all in." But now, a new identity loomed large, amorphous and intimidating: father.

Parenthood, as many discover, isn't a simple addition to one's résumé. It's a shift in gravitational pull, a rebalancing act that changes the way every other part of life fits together. Studies have shown that the experience of becoming a parent fundamentally alters the way we see ourselves and relate to the world around us. The journey from self-focused professional to parent is, at its core, an identity expansion, and few moments in life invite such a profound sense of duality. It is a challenging life transition, "particularly as it involves a process of renegotiating their repertoire of roles and identities to accommodate that of 'parent.'"[1] Specifically, this is a formative period, when the traditional gendered division of labor is often manifested and/or amplified,[2] and a time when the new parental identities are integrated into identity hierarchies within which multiple roles and identities (e.g., spouse, worker) already exist.[3] Furthermore, it is a restructuring period during which new parents often experience changes in their social networks (e.g., friendships) and associated social identities.[4]

The Identity Split: A Balancing Act

Sociologist Arlie Hochschild once wrote about the "second shift," describing the unpaid labor parents, especially mothers, face after their official workday ends. But the transformation starts earlier—before late-night feedings and school drop-offs—when expectant parents begin to feel a subtle but powerful tug at their sense of self.

For Ben, the realization hit during a casual lunch with his colleagues, when the conversation filled with buzzwords like "client strategy" and "Q4 projections." Midsentence, his phone vibrated with a text from his partner: "Just saw our baby kick during the ultrasound. Wish you were here." The disconnect between the two realities was palpable. Here he was, discussing branding campaigns, while a new, unseen chapter of his life unfolded elsewhere.

Ben's experience isn't unique. Many parents-to-be encounter this bifurcated reality: one foot remains firmly planted in their established professional world as the other steps tentatively into the unknown landscape of parenthood. Psychologist Erik Erikson's theory of psychosocial development posits that as we move through life stages, we constantly navigate tensions between opposing identities. For the working parent, the central tension is between the satisfaction of work and love for a child, or professional ambition and parental duty.

This isn't just a metaphorical struggle—it's a reality measured in cortisol spikes, midafternoon guilt, and whispered reassurances exchanged with partners during late-night talks. A survey conducted by the Pew Research Center found that more than 80 percent of working parents feel that they are never truly "off" from either role, navigating a psychological space where work and parenting blend and blur.[5]

Narratives of Change

Lisa, an architect who prides herself on her attention to detail, learned as a parent to leverage her work skills for her new home life. Lisa's days were once filled with blueprints, late-night emails, and the satisfaction of watching her designs take shape in the real world. The birth of her daughter introduced a new set of blueprints—ones that involved sleep schedules, pediatrician visits, and complicated logistics for even simple tasks like getting out of the house.

For the first few weeks, Lisa found herself resisting the new label of "mother," clinging to her professional identity as primary, as a sort of life raft in an uncharted sea. But gradually, something shifted. She began to recognize that the strategic thinking that made her successful at work was also her ally at home. Organizing a presentation for stakeholders wasn't all that different from coordinating a support network of friends and family, ensuring someone was always available to help. Lisa's story underscores a truth that many working parents come to learn: the skills honed in one domain can enrich the other.

In moments of crisis, this duality becomes most vivid. When a major client meeting coincided with her daughter's sudden fever, Lisa had to navigate her professional and personal priorities, and confront the reality that her two roles were sometimes at odds. It was during this time that she realized the dual identity wasn't a conflict but a balancing act—one that required constant recalibration. She would later describe this realization as akin to walking a tightrope with grace learned through experience and a measure of forgiveness toward oneself.

The Power of Reframing

What makes the identity shift that accompanies new parenthood transformative isn't just the act of juggling dual roles but an understanding that they can, in fact, complement each other. Though it sometimes appears that the parenting versus professional choices are zero-sum, that is rarely true. The dual identity is not an either–or proposition. It is, to borrow a concept from cognitive psychology, an exercise in reframing. Instead of viewing the demands of work and parenthood as opposing forces, what if we see them as complementary?

Research featured in *HR Magazine* indicates that becoming a parent can enhance workplace performance.[6] According to the research, 44 percent of working parents reported improved time management and organizational skills after having children. Additionally, 41 percent noted increased resilience, and 40 percent felt better equipped to manage their well-being. Parenthood also appeared to bolster leadership abilities, with 39 percent of respondents feeling more influential and 38 percent reporting enhanced leadership skills. These findings suggest that the experience of parenting cultivates transferable skills that positively impact professional effectiveness. For Lisa, this became evident during an intense project pitch. Her newfound ability to adapt on the fly, nurtured through countless nights adjusting to her daughter's unpredictable sleep cycle, made her a more flexible and resilient leader.

The power of reframing comes down to seeing value where others might see limitation. It is the realization that parenthood, with its unpredictability and emotional depth, is a training ground like no other for balancing priorities and making quick decisions; it is a psychological space where resilience is built, not merely tested. In an era when employers seek leaders who embody empathy and emotional intelligence, working parents find themselves uniquely equipped.

Emotional Preparation for Parenthood

Late one evening, Mira sat on the edge of her bed, staring at the nightstand cluttered with baby books, each title promising answers and reassurance. She was an attorney who thrived in high-stress courtrooms, where sharp instincts and preparation were her allies. Yet, in the quiet anticipation of her first child's arrival, the feeling gnawing at her wasn't something she could prepare for by reading. It was an uncharted blend of excitement, anxiety, and self-doubt—a landscape where even the most formidable professionals have found themselves unmoored.

The emotional preparation for parenthood is a journey laden with paradoxes. It is the anticipation of joy mixed with the dread of change; it is the thrill of new life intertwined with the fear of losing one's old self. For many expectant parents, this psychological terrain feels at once deeply personal and universally shared, an emotional balancing act that no amount of professional training can simulate.

The Anxiety–Excitement Spectrum

Consider the case of Jonathan, a seasoned tech firm project manager known for his methodical approach to life. When he and his partner learned they were expecting, Jonathan approached the news like any other major project. He outlined a detailed plan: a budget for baby expenses, a timeline for home renovations, and even a checklist of potential daycares ranked by location and ratings. Yet, as weeks turned into months, Jonathan realized that, unlike his meticulously managed projects, parenthood defied linear predictability.

The unpredictability is where anxiety finds fertile ground. Expectant parents, regardless of their socioeconomic status or experience, often face a unique type of anticipatory anxiety. This anxiety is not just about the tangible aspects of parenting—finances, time management, and logistics—but also about the shift in identity and the unknown impact on mental and emotional health.

Jonathan's precise spreadsheets couldn't answer the questions that kept him up at night: Would he be a good father? Could he balance late work hours with story time and midnight feedings? When faced with the ambiguity of what lay ahead, Jonathan's initial response was to double down on control. It wasn't until a colleague shared an offhand comment—"Parenthood isn't something you master; it's like a wave you learn to ride"—that Jonathan began to realize emotional preparation was not about erasing anxiety but learning to coexist with it.

The Cognitive Dissonance of Expectation

The emotional landscape of parenthood is fraught with cognitive dissonance—the psychological discomfort of holding contradictory beliefs. Parents-to-be often envision an idyllic version of themselves: endlessly patient, adept, and unfazed by the chaos of early parenthood. Yet, reality soon challenges these assumptions, creating tension between expectation and experience.

A poignant example of this tension came from Claire, a high-powered executive at a pharmaceutical company. Known for her composure during crisis negotiations, Claire assumed she would face parenthood with the same unflappable demeanor. But during a prenatal class, when the instructor discussed the sleep deprivation and emotional upheaval of the early months, Claire felt a pang of panic. The image of herself—cool, collected, and capable—wobbled. The class instructor, sensing her unease, said, "It's okay to be scared. The best parents I know are those who admit they don't have all the answers."

Claire's story highlights a crucial component of emotional preparation: reconciling the idealized vision of oneself with the reality of impending uncertainty. The process involves embracing vulnerability, a quality that is often undervalued in the workplace but essential in the parenting realm. In fact, research by Brené Brown, a leading expert on vulnerability, suggests that accepting emotional exposure is a sign of strength, not weakness.[7] For expectant parents, this means understanding that admitting fears or anxieties isn't a lapse in readiness but an integral step toward resilience.

Shared Stories and Strength in Community

One of the most profound, and often overlooked, elements of emotional preparation is the strength found in community. During pregnancy, Mira, the attorney from earlier, joined a prenatal yoga class—not because she particularly enjoyed yoga but because her doctor recommended it for stress management. What she didn't expect was the connection she found with the other women in the class. They were doctors, teachers, and entrepreneurs, all powerful in their respective fields yet equally vulnerable when discussing impending parenthood.

One evening after class, as rain drummed against the studio's windows, the women lingered, swapping stories of pregnancy cravings, irrational fears, and the things that kept them up at night. It was during these conversations that Mira found something she couldn't glean from a book or an article: shared experience. Hearing that others felt the same mix of anticipation and apprehension helped Mira reframe her emotional state. She wasn't failing to prepare; she was, simply, preparing in the only way one could—by leaning into the experience and accepting the emotions as they came.

Sociologists have long noted that shared experiences can mitigate feelings of isolation and build a collective sense of normalcy. As we will discuss in a later chapter, this is where an Employee Resource Group (ERG) for parents can provide much-needed emotional support in the workplace. Research from the Centers for Disease Control and Prevention (CDC) and the University of Michigan has found that expectant parents who participated in support groups reported higher levels of emotional readiness and lower levels of postpartum anxiety.[8] These findings underscore a simple truth: emotional preparation isn't done in isolation. It thrives in community, in the moments when one's worries are met with nods of recognition and words of empathy. It is easy to see the parallels to healthy workplace team dynamics: parenting and effective teamwork both require the ability to connect with others and rely on the value of empathy and cooperation. These emerging perspectives and skills are ones that bridge the gap between parenthood and the workplace. As we further describe below, there are others, and they define the parenthood advantage.

The Anticipation of Ambiguity

Perhaps one of the most paradoxical lessons for expectant parents is learning to anticipate ambiguity. John Keats, the Romantic poet, coined the term "negative capability," the ability to hold uncertainty and doubt without the urgent need to resolve them. In many ways, preparing emotionally for parenthood requires developing this very skill.

Take Ravi and Priya, a couple who both worked as engineers at the same firm. Logical, precise, and highly organized, they approached life with an engineer's mentality. Yet, as their due date approached, Priya confessed to Ravi during a walk in the park, "I'm terrified that we're about to enter a part of life where logic won't always apply." Ravi nodded, feeling the weight of her words settle between them. It was true—no spreadsheet or to-do list could prepare them for the sleepless nights or the rush of love and exhaustion that everyone said would arrive in equal measure.

The weeks leading up to the birth were filled with moments that tested their ability to sit with uncertainty: a scan that came back inconclusive, a change in their doctor's availability, and the inevitable realization that their well-rehearsed birth plan might not play out as expected. Yet, with each unexpected twist, Ravi and Priya found themselves growing more comfortable with the ambiguity. They learned to pause, breathe, and remind each other that not everything needed an immediate solution, a thoughtful approach that can easily be applied to the workplace.

Embracing the Unknown

In the final weeks before Mira's baby was due, she found herself again staring at the books on her nightstand. But this time, she felt different. The pages no longer represented answers she needed but stories that confirmed she was already on the right path. Parenthood, she realized, was not about conquering fear but living with it and letting it transform into something else—love, readiness, and the resilience to face whatever came next.

Emotional preparation is, in many ways, an act of faith. It is believing that, despite the moments of doubt and the quiet tremors of anxiety, you will meet the challenges as they come. It's about understanding that every parent begins this journey from the same place: with questions, fears, and an open heart.

Balancing Work–Life Anticipation and Reality

In the months leading up to her due date, Emily, a senior marketing executive, could not shake the feeling of impending transformation. A high achiever by any standard, she'd risen quickly in her career, earning accolades for her creativity and strategic foresight. But as her pregnancy advanced, so, too, did the growing weight of the question that had started to gnaw at her: *How will I balance work and motherhood?* This fear was exacerbated by the fact that Emily was going through her pregnancy, and probably the first part of her child's life, as a single parent.

For Emily, like many, balancing work and life seemed like a solvable puzzle, one that she could approach with the same precision and planning she applied to her career. She read articles, listened to podcasts, and even attended workshops on how to manage life as a working parent. She believed that with enough time management and preparation, the transition into motherhood would be as seamless as any successful project. Yet, as Emily would soon learn, balancing work and life with an infant is often far messier, more complex, and infinitely more unpredictable than her preconceptions had prepared her for.

The Idealized Balance: A Flawed Blueprint

The narrative of "having it all" has long permeated popular culture, dominated by the image of the successful parent who manages to juggle career demands, family needs, and self-care with grace. It's the ideal that many expectant parents, especially those in high-pressure careers, aspire to. Books like *Lean In* by Sheryl Sandberg and *The Five-Hour Workday* by Stephan Aarstol, though well-meaning, have propagated the belief that, with discipline and perseverance, one can achieve the perfect work–life equilibrium.

But when reality sets in, these models of balance often fail to account for the unpredictability and complexity of real-life parenting. What happens when an urgent project at work coincides with your child's first fever? Or when you've just started a high-stakes meeting only to realize your daycare provider called in sick? The theoretical balance of work and life becomes distorted in moments like these, when the stark reality of competing priorities takes center stage.

Take, for example, Robert and Linda, a couple who both worked demanding jobs in finance. Robert was a senior analyst at a well-known investment firm, while Linda was an entry-level associate at a major tech company. Before their child was born, they shared the belief that they could "have it all"—after all, they had mastered the art of balancing work deadlines with personal commitments. But when their baby arrived, Linda found herself overwhelmed by the reality of breastfeeding schedules, sleepless nights, and the constant tug-of-war between her work obligations and the needs of her newborn. Robert, though he tried to be supportive, found himself increasingly frustrated by the unpredictable nature of their home life. The carefully planned, predictable rhythms of their pre-parenthood life seemed impossible to re-create in the whirlwind of daily parenting.

Psychologists have long observed that there's a cognitive dissonance between the "ideal" work–life balance and the reality that most people experience. A recent article highlights the growing emotional toll of work–family conflict for parents. Nearly a third (29 percent) of working parents are experiencing high or extreme levels of stress.[9] Among those reporting high stress levels, four in five (80 percent) said the strain made it difficult to concentrate at work. In another study—the *Modern Families Index 2025* by Bright Horizons—also revealed that nearly three quarters (72 percent) of these highly stressed parents described their daily experience as "completely overwhelming."[10] This gap between expectation and reality can lead to burnout, guilt, and resentment, emotions that Emily, Robert, and Linda would all come to recognize.

The New Reality: Disruption and Adaptation

The truth is that work–life balance isn't static. It is dynamic, fluctuating, and subject to constant change. In her life "pre-baby," Emily had responded to both challenges and opportunities by simply working harder and longer. But when she returned to work after her maternity leave, she quickly realized that her carefully constructed plans for balance were no match for the daily, unpredictable demands of motherhood. Her first week back was a blur of conference calls, client presentations, and the ever-present reminder of her newborn's needs at home. She had expected to be able to "turn off" the stress of her job when she stepped into her role as a mother, but instead, she found herself stretched thin in both arenas.

One day, after a particularly draining twelve-hour workday, Emily came home to find her baby crying and inconsolable. The two worlds collided in an agonizing moment of realization: she couldn't simply divide her attention between the demands of work and motherhood. Her expectation that she could maintain the same level of focus and productivity at work while being the doting mother she envisioned was being tested by the demands of reality.

Emily's experience is not unique. It echoes the challenges faced by many working parents—especially mothers, who continue to bear the brunt of caregiving responsibilities. A study from the Pew Research Center found that women are still more likely than men to handle daily household duties, even when both parents work full-time.[11] This "second shift" often leads to an increased feeling of imbalance and inequity, with women reporting higher levels of stress related to the competing demands of career and family.

From Balance to Integration

But while the challenge of balancing work and life is undeniable, it is also an opportunity for adaptation. Emily, like many parents, began to recalibrate her expectations, learning to forgive herself for the times when she couldn't be the perfect employee or the perfect parent. She began to let go of the ideal of perfect balance and instead focused on the concept of "work–life integration," a term used to describe a more fluid, adaptive approach to managing professional and personal commitments.

This shift in mindset—from balance to integration—allowed Emily to build a more sustainable routine. Instead of rigidly compartmentalizing her work and personal life, she began to allow space for the fluidity of both. She started setting boundaries at work, saying no to nonessential meetings and prioritizing flexibility in her schedule. At home, she worked to create a network of helpers, including paid caregivers and family and friends, which allowed her to accommodate her baby's needs without sacrificing her own well-being.

The idea of work–life integration is gaining traction in corporate culture as well. Companies like Google and Patagonia have been at the forefront of offering flexible work schedules, on-site childcare, and generous parental leave policies to support their employees' needs. This approach acknowledges that work and personal life are not separate entities but interconnected parts of a whole. As Emily's experience shows, integrating these aspects of life is far more achievable than trying to balance them perfectly.

Embracing Growth and Self-Compassion

When a child is born, so too is a new version of yourself. The transformation is not just physical—though, certainly for birthing parents, the changes in your body are undeniable—but psychological, emotional, and social. Parenthood rewrites the narrative of who you are. It forces you to reckon with your ideals, to question your expectations, and—perhaps most importantly—to embrace the discomfort of change. The ideal of "having it all" fades into the background, and in its place a more fluid, complex, and often more rewarding path emerges. This path, though fraught with challenges, can also lead to profound growth, but it requires something that tends to be overlooked in our culture of achievement: self-compassion.

In her book *The Gifts of Imperfection*, Brené Brown speaks to the heart of this journey, noting that "You are imperfect, you are wired for struggle, but you are worthy of love and belonging." This notion of imperfection—of accepting ourselves as we are rather than chasing an unattainable ideal—is perhaps one of the most crucial lessons for working parents to internalize. Parenthood, like no other life stage, holds a mirror up to our vulnerabilities, our limitations, and our ability to adapt. The question then becomes: How do we respond to the mirror? Do we embrace the reflection, with all its messiness and humanity, or do we continue to chase the ghost of the perfect parent, the ideal worker, the flawless partner?

The Paradox of Parenthood and Growth

The irony of parenting is that, while it is undoubtedly one of the most challenging experiences of any adult's life, it offers the opportunity for tremendous growth. But growth, by its very nature, requires discomfort. It requires pushing past the boundaries of what we thought we were capable of. And for most parents, this is where the struggle begins.

Jessica is a project manager at a tech company. Before having her first child, she had been known for her impeccable work ethic. She was organized, punctual, and always ahead of the curve. Her career trajectory was on an upward climb, and she had all but mastered the art of balancing her personal life with her professional responsibilities. But after her child was born, the dynamics of her life shifted in ways she hadn't anticipated. The sleep deprivation, constant juggling of competing priorities, and overwhelming need to be "on" at work while being fully present at home started to wear on her.

At first, Jessica fought the change. She kept pushing herself to maintain the same level of productivity at work, the same level of engagement with her child, and the same sense of control over her personal life. But after a few months, it became clear that something had to give. Jessica's performance at work started to slip. Because the transitions in her life were real but support structures for her new reality were not firmly in place, Jessica was not fully prepared to manage her return to work effectively. She missed deadlines, her presentations were less polished, and her contributions at meetings seemed scattered. Her home life, too, was buckling under the strain. She was irritable, exhausted, and, most painfully, she felt disconnected from her baby during the too-infrequent moments they spent together.

Jessica's employer offered parental leave without any additional resources. There was no guidance on her exit plan before her leave, no check-ins during her leave, and no plan for her return to work except the date she would resume all of her normal responsibilities. Jessica worked for a fast-moving company that valued her as a contributing employee but failed to comprehend her experience as a new parent. They treated her exactly the way they might treat someone who took a long vacation. Without parenting ERGs, there was an absence of community, and the company made no attempt to connect new parents who were going through the same struggles. As Jessica's work and life challenges increased, her uneven performance played into the cultural stereotype of women as less desirable employees after they have children. The situation also made Jessica doubt herself.

Not until she had a candid conversation with a colleague—a fellow parent who had gone through similar struggles—did Jessica realize the truth: she wasn't failing; she was growing. Her sense of self-worth had been tied to her ability to meet pre-parenthood standards, but those standards were no longer realistic. Jessica had to redefine what success looked like for her in this new phase of life. She learned to take breaks, to delegate, and to ask for help. And most importantly, she learned to practice self-compassion.

She stopped berating herself for not being perfect and began embracing the messy and imperfect but beautiful reality of being both a parent and a professional.

The conversation with her colleague increased her awareness that creating connections with others was a huge value add, so she started an ad hoc new-parents lunch group. The first week, three female colleagues joined her. By the end of the month, the group had grown to twenty men and women. They realized that they shared common struggles that could be addressed by some simple corporate actions.

Jessica's increased empathy as a parent enhanced her ability to connect with others at work and built her ability to be more compassionate with herself. The parenting group coordinated with Learning and Development (L&D) to bring in a speaker on self-compassion, which benefited all employees. Self-compassion, as psychologist Kristin Neff has outlined, is the ability to treat oneself with kindness in times of failure, struggle, or pain. It is not about excusing mistakes or lowering standards but rather about acknowledging that suffering and imperfection are part of the human experience. For parents, this can be a radical shift, especially given a wider culture that often equates success with flawless execution.

Jessica's story is not unique. It is a narrative shared by many parents, especially those who experience the pressure to excel both at work and at home. The societal narrative of "having it all" suggests that working parents should be able to manage both spheres seamlessly, but the reality is that no one can. The key, instead, is to embrace imperfection and to lean into the process of growth, rather than pursuing an unrealistic ideal of perfection.

Take, for example, Marcus, an accountant who became a father while managing a high-stress job. The first few months of parenthood were brutal for him. His wife returned to her job shortly after their child was born. Marcus could work from home, so he took on the role of primary caregiver. Marcus tried to juggle the early days of fatherhood alongside the ever-present demands of his career. He tried to keep the same pace at his job, working late into the evening to meet deadlines, all while taking on the daytime childcare responsibilities. As the weeks went by, Marcus grew increasingly irritable, stressed, and withdrawn. It wasn't until he read an article about self-compassion in a *Harvard Business Review* newsletter that he realized he was at a breaking point.

Inspired by the research, Marcus began to implement small but profound changes. He and his wife, who faced a similar work and life struggle, had more frank conversations about balancing the role as co-parents. He began to allow himself to shut down work at scheduled times, which was difficult because it was always present in his home. He created physical boundaries, including keeping his laptop out of the nursery. Marcus reached out to his corporate Employee Assistance Program (EAP) to help him handle his new life. He also reached out to a colleague, who became his accountability partner, reminding him that he didn't have to be perfect and that asking for help wasn't a sign of weakness but rather of strength. Over time, Marcus learned to accept the ebb and flow of his work–life balance. There were good days and bad days, but he no longer held himself to the unattainable standard of "doing it all." He embraced his growth and gave himself permission to be imperfect.

Neff's research also highlights the link between self-compassion and resilience. When parents are kind to themselves, they are better able to recover from setbacks and stay motivated through challenges. Marcus, like many other parents, discovered that when he stopped seeing his struggles as failures, he was able to recover more quickly and with greater strength. He learned that the road to success is not linear, but rather a winding path that requires both persistence and forgiveness.

The Role of Growth in Career Development

While self-compassion is crucial to navigating the early days of parenthood, it also has long-term implications for career growth. The pressure to "bounce back" after having a child often leads parents, especially mothers, to question their professional trajectory. They may worry that taking time off or adjusting their work schedule will hinder their career advancement. But studies have shown that parents who embrace the growth opportunities inherent in balancing work and family often develop crucial skills that benefit their careers in the long run.

A McKinsey & Company survey highlights how parental leave—particularly paternity leave—can generate benefits that extend beyond personal well-being and into the workplace.[12] Fathers who take leave often return to work with improved communication skills, increased empathy, and a greater capacity for balancing competing demands. These experiences help foster qualities like emotional intelligence, adaptability, and problem solving—traits that are critical in today's complex work environments. As McKinsey notes, encouraging parental leave for all caregivers can build more inclusive workplaces and develop leaders who are more attuned to the human side of management. For many working parents, the skills they develop in their personal lives often spill over into their professional lives, creating a more balanced and adaptive approach to their careers.

The process of embracing growth and self-compassion is not an easy one. It requires a radical shift in the way we view success—not as a static state of perfection but as a dynamic process that allows for both growth and failure. Parenthood, more than any other experience, forces us to confront our limitations and rethink our assumptions about what it means to "succeed." But it is through this discomfort that we discover the depth of our resilience, the power of our adaptability, and the richness of our lives.

In the end, the path to success—as a parent and as a professional—is not defined by a perfect balance of work and life. It is defined by our ability to adapt, embrace our imperfections, and give ourselves permission to grow. The more we learn to embrace this growth with compassion, the more we can thrive in both our personal and professional lives.

Conclusion: Navigating the Shift, Embracing the Growth

The transition to parenthood marks one of the most profound identity shifts in adult life. It challenges everything we thought we knew about ourselves—our priorities, our limitations, and our definition of success. Far from being a simple juggling act, becoming a working parent is an ongoing negotiation between competing identities and evolving roles.

This chapter has explored how that psychological shift impacts not only personal well-being but professional performance, often in surprising ways. Parenthood cultivates resilience, emotional intelligence, and adaptability, traits that enrich our contributions at work as much as they shape our growth at home. Yet these gains are often obscured by outdated narratives and workplace norms that pit career ambition against caregiving.

What emerges as we examine the data and the lived realities of new parents is a more nuanced truth: that identity as a parent and identity as a professional are not in conflict but in conversation. Navigating that conversation requires support, reflection, and, above all, self-compassion.

For individuals, the challenge is to embrace this complexity with flexibility and grace. For organizations, the opportunity is to recognize the value of the parental experience and to build cultures that support, rather than sideline, this evolution. Parenthood doesn't diminish our professional selves—it expands them. And when both employees and employers understand that truth, we don't just retain talent—we unlock it.

Key Takeaways

- **Becoming a parent initiates a profound shift in identity.** This shift requires individuals to continually reconcile and integrate their roles as both professionals and caregivers.
- **Emotional preparation for parenthood means learning to accept uncertainty.** Adjusting expectations and approaching the transition with self-compassion are critical.
- **The roles of parent and professional can strengthen each other.** Approached with intention and flexibility, the roles complement rather than conflict.
- **A discrepancy between what we expect from parenthood and what we experience is normal.** Developing the ability to adapt is essential to well-being and healthy growth.
- **We must give ourselves permission to be imperfect.** When we do, parenthood becomes a powerful catalyst for both personal and professional growth.

Reflection

1. How do you anticipate your identity will shift as you transition into parenthood?
2. What strategies can you adopt to manage the emotional and practical challenges of this life change?
3. How do you see your role as a parent enhancing your professional capabilities, and vice versa?
4. What areas of your work–life balance do you feel most concerned about? How might you proactively address these concerns?
5. Reflect on a time when you faced a major life transition. What lessons from that experience could you apply to your journey into parenthood?

5 | BOUNDARIES AND BALANCE

At a fast-growing software company we will call Brightwave Tech, parental leave was officially supported, but in practice, employees had vastly different experiences depending on their manager's approach. There was no systemic policy guiding how managers should handle leave transitions, and as a result, some employees were able to fully disconnect while others found themselves tethered to work even when they were supposed to be away.

Two Different Paths

When Aisha, a senior marketing strategist, announced her pregnancy to her manager, Ian, he assured her that the company valued work–life balance and that she should take the time she needed. They briefly discussed a transition plan, and Ian reassured her that if anything urgent came up, they'd try to handle it—but they might need her insight from time to time.

Aisha was pleased that the team saw her value and she appreciated being apprised of major developments, but expectations had not been outlined clearly and the boundary was difficult to manage. Just a few weeks into her leave, as she was beginning to recover from the birth and establish a routine at home, Aisha started receiving messages from her team. A junior colleague struggled with a campaign and reached out for "quick input." Then Ian forwarded an email about an upcoming product launch, saying, "No pressure—just keeping you in the loop." Wanting to support her team, Aisha responded. At first, the messages were occasional, but soon she found herself checking her email and answering Slack messages daily, and even taking a few calls.

By the time she returned, Aisha felt like she had never truly been away. Instead of returning refreshed, she felt burned out and overwhelmed. Worse, because she had stayed involved, her team had not fully adjusted in her absence, leaving a backlog of work that now fell squarely on her shoulders. Within six months, she began quietly looking for a new job, one at which parental leave was truly protected.

Meanwhile, Margie, a product manager in another division, was also preparing for parental leave. Margie's manager, Elena, unlike Ian, took a more structured approach. Before Margie's leave, Elena set up a detailed transition plan, redistributed key responsibilities, and designated a single point of contact for any work-related questions.

Elena made it clear: "You are off the grid. We will not reach out, and we don't expect you to check in. Your job is to focus on your family. We've got this."

Instead of sporadic emails and subtle pressures, Margie received only one pre-agreed update at the halfway point of her leave—purely for her awareness, with no action required. Her team adapted in her absence, stepping into new responsibilities and developing skills they otherwise wouldn't have.

When Margie returned, she was fully recharged and ready to contribute. She found that her team had grown in confidence, and she wasn't burdened with cleaning up unresolved issues. The seamless transition made her feel valued and reinforced her commitment to Brightwave Tech.

The Hidden Problem:
Uneven Experiences Drive Talent Away

Both Aisha and Margie worked at the same company, but because Brightwave Tech lacked a clear, company-wide parental leave process and robust manager training, the employees' experiences were entirely dependent on the leadership styles of their managers.

Aisha's experience left her feeling exhausted and disengaged, while Margie returned energized and committed, thanks to her manager's proactive approach. The inconsistency created frustration among employees, who saw that some colleagues were fully supported while others were expected to "stay in the loop." Without a standardized approach, Brightwave Tech risked losing top talent—not because of bad policies but because of uneven execution.

The Manager's Role in Defining Boundaries

When an employee announces they are expecting a child, a manager's first instinct is often to focus on logistics: who will cover the employee's responsibilities, how long they will be away, and what their return might look like. But beyond these practical concerns lies a far more significant responsibility: ensuring that the employee's parental leave is truly protected.

Without clear boundaries, parental leave can easily become a blurred space where work obligations creep in. An email here, a "quick" check-in there, a request to weigh in on a project—it all adds up. Slowly, the expectation of complete disengagement erodes, and the employee finds themselves mentally tethered to their job at a time when their focus should be elsewhere. The impact of this is twofold: the employee loses the opportunity to fully embrace the profound transition to parenthood, and the company risks a depleted and disengaged team member upon their return.

Conversely, when boundaries are well-defined and actively respected, employees come back to work more engaged, focused, and ready to contribute. Parental leave is not just an extended out-of-office message; it is a period of intense personal transformation that should not be encroached upon.

Setting the Tone for Parental Leave

A manager's approach to parental leave sets the tone for the rest of the organization. If a leader reaches out to an employee on leave "just to check in" or subtly implies that their input would still be valuable, they create an unspoken expectation that availability is required. But if that same leader instead emphasizes the importance of complete disengagement and models that commitment by respecting the leave boundary, they signal to the entire team that this time is truly sacred.

Before an employee steps away, manager and employee must have a structured conversation that lays the groundwork for their absence and eventual return. Together, they should clarify how responsibilities will be transitioned, who will handle key projects, and how (or if) the employee would like to receive any updates. Some people prefer total detachment, while others may want occasional check-ins at set intervals. What matters most is that the decision is intentional and employee-driven, rather than an assumption made by the organization.

Clear communication boundaries should be established from the outset. Employees should not feel obligated to monitor email, respond to messages, or stay involved in ongoing work. A well-designed leave policy makes it explicit that no work-related engagement is expected. In some companies, this is formalized through a "zero-expectation email" practice, where updates may be sent for reference but with no assumption that the employee will read or respond. Others opt for milestone check-ins at key points in the leave period, but only if the employee opts in. These choices empower employees to set the level of engagement that best suits their needs, rather than feeling pressured to stay connected out of fear of missing something important.

Just as important as defining these boundaries is ensuring that they are upheld. Employees take their cues from leadership, and if managers fail to respect parental leave, the message trickles down through the organization. An employee on leave who is cc'd on an email may feel an unspoken obligation to respond, even if no one directly asks them to. This is why modeling boundary setting is so essential. If a company truly values parental leave, leaders must be the first to enforce it, ensuring that employees feel safe stepping away.

One of the simplest yet most effective ways to reinforce this commitment is through clear, intentional messaging. An employee's out-of-office reply should state explicitly that they are on parental leave, that they will not be checking messages, and that any urgent matters should be directed to a designated colleague. This clarity eliminates any gray areas and prevents unnecessary disruptions. A strong organizational culture will support these boundaries by holding the line—not just in policy but in practice.

Why Boundaries and Communication Matter

Supporting parental leave isn't just a gesture of goodwill—it's a strategic investment in retention, engagement, and team development. Employees who can truly unplug during leave are more likely to return committed, energized, and ready to contribute, while those who remain tethered to work risk burnout and eventual attrition. Managers play a central role in this dynamic. By establishing clear boundaries and communicating expectations upfront, they reduce uncertainty, reinforce the employee's value, and prevent unnecessary stress. A thoughtful communication plan ensures that the employee can step away with confidence and return to a workplace that is organized, informed, and welcoming—not one that punishes them for their absence. When managers model and protect these norms, the entire organization benefits.

Breaking the Always-On Cycle: What Leaders Must Do

Managers have a unique opportunity—and responsibility—to break the cycle that demands employees be always "on." Simply having a parental leave policy is not enough; the real challenge is ensuring that it is honored in practice. That requires deliberate action and cultural change at the leadership level.

The problem is not unique to working parents. A 2021 *Harvard Business Review* study found that over 50 percent of employees across industries felt pressure to be available outside of standard working hours, even when their official company policies promoted work–life balance.[1] For new parents, this expectation is even more acute. A 2020 CNBC article reported that working mothers are 28 percent more likely to experience burnout than working fathers, highlighting the disproportionate challenges faced by women in balancing professional and personal responsibilities.[2]

One of the most effective ways to dismantle the "always-on" expectation is through visible leadership buy-in. If senior leaders take their own leave and model true disconnection, they signal to the entire organization that the benefit is not just theoretical—it's a respected and expected part of the employee experience. When executives set clear boundaries and respect them, they normalize the practice at all levels.

Companies must also put guardrails in place to ensure that employees are not subtly pressured to remain engaged. This means:

- Establishing explicit policies that prohibit contacting employees on leave except in true emergencies.
- Encouraging team-wide discussions before an employee departs, reinforcing that their responsibilities will be fully covered so they don't feel the need to check in.
- Monitoring the behavior of direct managers, ensuring they are not undermining policies by casually reaching out or expecting responsiveness.

Technology can also be leveraged to reinforce these boundaries. Some companies implement email and Slack blockers, preventing messages from being sent to employees on leave, while others use temporary account deactivation to ensure that employees aren't tempted to check in. While these tools can't replace cultural change, they serve as practical reinforcements of a company's commitment to work–life balance.

The Bottom Line: Performance Should Be Measured by Impact, Not Availability

The root of the always-on problem lies in the way performance is evaluated. Many workplaces still equate dedication with responsiveness rather than with meaningful contributions. Until this mindset shifts, employees—especially parents—will continue to feel pressure to be constantly available, even at the expense of their health and well-being.

For businesses, this is more than just an employee well-being issue—it's a productivity problem. Stanford University research on workplace efficiency found that employees who consistently work beyond normal hours experience a drop in productivity by up to 50 percent, as exhaustion and stress erode their ability to focus and make effective decisions.[3] Yet many companies still operate under the false assumption that more hours equal more output, an expectation that is particularly damaging for new parents trying to establish a sustainable routine.

Companies that measure success by impact rather than hours worked create an environment where employees feel empowered to set boundaries without fear of professional consequences. When performance is based on outcomes rather than presence, employees are free to fully embrace parental leave, return to work on a structured, sustainable timeline, and integrate their professional and personal lives in a way that benefits both them and their employer.

At its core, breaking free from an always-on culture requires a fundamental shift in how we define commitment, productivity, and leadership. It's not about working more hours, responding to emails at all times, or sacrificing personal life for professional gain. It's about creating a workplace where employees are valued for the quality of their work, not their constant availability—and where new parents can step away, return, and thrive without feeling like they need to prove their worth by being perpetually "on."

Reentry as a Boundary Moment

Returning from parental leave is among the most vulnerable stages in the working parent's journey. Employees come back changed—mentally and emotionally, and with a new set of logistical challenges—yet workplaces often treat the return as a simple handoff, expecting business as usual. This mismatch can create significant tension, especially when managers fail to recognize the return as a moment that requires both empathy and structure.

For many new parents, reentry is not about "picking up where they left off" but learning how to navigate a new dual identity in real time. Without thoughtful planning and clear boundaries, employees may feel either overwhelmed by an unmanageable workload or sidelined from meaningful opportunities—either of which can lead to disengagement and attrition.

That's why the return to work must be treated not as a one-day event but as a phased process. It begins with setting realistic expectations and communicating openly about what the employee needs to be successful in this new chapter. Flexibility, clarity of role, and cultural messaging that normalize the adjustment period are essential. Managers who proactively support this process are not only protecting the well-being of their employees, they are reinforcing loyalty and preserving valuable talent.

We will explore the concept of a structured "returnship" in more detail in a later chapter. For now, it's important to understand that a successful return isn't about seamless reintegration; it's about a supported, intentional transition that respects the boundaries and realities of new parenthood.

Setting and Enforcing Clear Time Boundaries

One of the simplest yet most effective ways to support new parents is to establish defined work hours and ensure they are respected. This means making it explicit that:

- Employees are not expected to respond to messages outside their designated working hours.
- Meetings should be scheduled within core working hours, avoiding times that interfere with caregiving responsibilities.
- Workloads should be realistic and manageable within standard working hours, rather than assuming employees will "catch up" in the evenings or on weekends.

While these policies may seem straightforward, enforcement is key. If a company says it values work–life balance but managers routinely send late-night emails, the message is clear: availability is still expected. Leaders must model the behavior they want to see, which means setting and respecting boundaries themselves.

A 2023 Deloitte report found that 84 percent of C-suite leaders believe employees are more likely to prioritize their own well-being when they see their company's executives doing the same, highlighting the powerful role of leadership in shaping a healthy workplace culture.[4] When leaders do not respond to emails after hours, avoid weekend work, and prioritize personal time, employees are more likely to do the same. In contrast, in organizations where leadership ignores these boundaries, employees report significantly higher levels of stress and lower job satisfaction.

Reforming Meeting Culture for Working Parents

One of the most overlooked aspects of work–life balance is meeting culture. In many workplaces, excessive meetings not only eat into productive time but also make it nearly impossible for parents to maintain a structured schedule. A 2022 report by Atlassian found that employees spend an average of thirty-one hours per month in unproductive meetings, with many of these meetings scheduled outside core working hours.[5]

For returning parents, meeting overload can be particularly frustrating. When meetings are scheduled at random hours, employees are forced to constantly rearrange their schedules, creating unnecessary stress and disruption, particularly for parents.

A better approach is to establish meeting discipline, ensuring that:

- Meetings are scheduled within predictable time blocks that accommodate all employees, including parents.
- Agendas are set in advance, so meetings stay focused and efficient.
- Only necessary participants are included, reducing wasted time.
- Asynchronous communication is used whenever possible, allowing parents to engage without being forced into unnecessary live meetings.

Companies like Shopify and Asana have successfully implemented "No Meeting Wednesdays" or designated "Core Meeting Hours" policies, ensuring that employees have uninterrupted work time and that meetings do not encroach on personal boundaries.

Respecting Time Boundaries Creates a Competitive Advantage

Organizations that protect and enforce time boundaries don't just create happier employees, they gain a strategic advantage. Companies that prioritize work–life balance report higher retention rates, stronger employee engagement, and increased productivity.

One striking example comes from Salesforce, which implemented a series of work–life balance initiatives, including defined working hours and flexible scheduling. The result? Employee satisfaction scores increased by 16 percent, and attrition rates among working parents dropped by 40 percent.

In contrast, companies that fail to enforce time boundaries often experience higher turnover. According to SHRM's 2024 *Burnout* report, employees experiencing burnout are nearly three times more likely to be actively searching for another job, highlighting the powerful connection between burnout and workforce turnover.[6]

For managers, the takeaway is clear: employees who are given well-defined, respected time boundaries are more engaged, more productive, and more likely to stay. When working parents know that their time is valued, they can contribute at a high level without the constant stress of being "always available."

The Role of Leadership in Shaping Time Culture

At the heart of effective time boundaries is leadership accountability. It is not enough for a company to have policies on paper—leaders must actively create a culture where work is structured around sustainable schedules rather than constant availability.

This means:

- Encouraging employees to log off at the end of their workday without guilt or penalty.
- Not rewarding overwork—avoiding the tendency to see long hours as a sign of dedication.
- Ensuring that performance evaluations reflect contributions, not presence or responsiveness.

A strong culture of time discipline doesn't just benefit working parents—it benefits everyone. Employees who feel empowered to set boundaries are more productive, less likely to burn out, and more committed to their roles.

At the end of the day, the goal is not just to help parents navigate work–life balance but to build an organization where balance is the norm, not the exception. By protecting time boundaries, companies don't just retain talent—they create a workplace where employees can thrive, no matter their stage of life.

Rethinking Flexibility:
Beyond "Work from Home"

Over the past decade, workplace flexibility has been hailed as the ultimate solution for work–life balance, particularly for parents. The rise of remote work—accelerated by the COVID-19 pandemic—was seen as a major win for working families, offering the freedom to manage professional and personal responsibilities more seamlessly. But for many parents, the reality of "flexibility" has been far more complicated.

While remote- and hybrid-work options certainly provide greater autonomy, they do not automatically equate to true balance. In fact, a 2023 report by the National Bureau of Economic Research (NBER) found that remote workers work 9.2 percent longer hours on average than their in-office counterparts, largely because the lines between work and home become increasingly blurred.[7]

For new parents, this dynamic is even more challenging. Instead of creating balance, remote work often leads to pervasive work creep, leading employees to feel compelled to be available at all hours, struggle to set clear work–home boundaries, and ultimately experience higher stress and burnout. A 2023 Gallup report found that fully remote workers are more likely to experience daily stress—45 percent compared to 38–39 percent of on-site workers—largely due to isolation, autonomy-related pressures, and the difficulty of maintaining clear boundaries between work and personal life.[8]

These findings underscore a critical point: flexibility is not just about location—it's about control over one's time, workload, and ability to disconnect. To truly support working parents, companies must move beyond the simplistic notion of "work from home" and instead design intentional, structured flexibility that actually promotes balance.

The Difference Between Structured and Unstructured Flexibility

Not all flexibility is created equal. Many companies offer hybrid or remote options without implementing the policies needed to prevent overwork, enforce boundaries, and ensure that flexibility does not come at the cost of career advancement.

Unstructured flexibility—where employees are expected to "figure it out" on their own—often backfires. Without clear guardrails, parents may feel pressure to be constantly available, to prove they are still fully committed despite not being physically present in the office. In contrast, companies that implement structured flexibility—where expectations are clear, work is measured by output rather than presence, and flexibility is intentionally designed to support work–life integration—see far better outcomes. Employees in these environments report higher job satisfaction, lower burnout rates, and greater loyalty to their employers.

Designing Flexibility That Works for Working Parents

For flexibility to be truly effective, it must be intentional, well-structured, and reinforced by company culture. The most successful companies go beyond simply offering remote work and instead implement policies that ensure flexibility translates into real balance.

Some of the most effective approaches include:

- **Core work hours instead of an "always available" culture.** Many companies now define core collaboration hours (e.g., 10 a.m. to 3 p.m.), allowing employees to schedule their day around those key windows while maintaining flexibility for the rest of their work. This approach provides structure while still accommodating caregiving responsibilities.
- **Results-oriented performance metrics.** Companies that evaluate employees based on outcomes rather than hours worked create an environment where flexibility is genuinely respected. This approach shifts the focus from face time to actual contributions, reducing the pressure to be constantly visible and available.
- **Predictable, transparent scheduling policies.** For flexibility to work, employees need predictability— especially parents managing childcare logistics. Some companies implement predictable scheduling commitments, where meetings are clustered within certain hours and work expectations outside of those windows are minimized.

- **Job-sharing and reduced-hour leadership tracks.** One of the biggest obstacles for working parents—particularly mothers—is the assumption that flexibility means stepping back from leadership. However, forward-thinking companies are proving that reduced-hour roles and job-sharing arrangements can work at even the highest levels.

The Future of Flexibility: What Managers Must Do Now

For managers, as we've laid out, the shift toward effective flexibility requires rethinking the way work is structured, performance is evaluated, and employees are supported.

At an individual level, to make flexibility work in practice, managers should:

- Have structured, proactive conversations about what flexibility means for each employee.
- Align flexibility with business priorities, ensuring that employees can contribute meaningfully without sacrificing balance.
- Monitor and correct any bias that penalizes employees who take advantage of flexible policies.
- Lead by example, modeling boundaries and demonstrating that flexibility is not just allowed, but valued.

At its core, flexibility should empower employees, not burden them with additional stress. Companies that get this right will not only attract and retain top talent but also create a more resilient, engaged, and high-performing workforce.

We are describing flexibility here in the context of working parents. As you see in other parts of this book, when discussing issues for parents, it is instructive to consider the corollary identity: nonparents. To counter the concerns of nonparents who sometimes feel overburdened to "pick up the slack" of working parents, flexibility should become a core part of an organization's culture. It should extend to everyone.

In the future of work, flexibility will not be a perk—it will be the defining factor of successful, sustainable workplaces. For businesses looking to stay competitive, the time to move beyond "work from home" and into true, structured flexibility is now.

The Role of Culture in Sustaining Boundaries

Policies and programs can define the framework for work–life balance, but culture is what determines whether they truly work. A company may offer parental leave, flexible work arrangements, or structured boundaries around time off, but if the prevailing culture still rewards overwork, glorifies constant availability, and stigmatizes those who take advantage of these policies, employees will hesitate to use them.

This tension between stated policies and cultural reality is one of the biggest obstacles to creating sustainable work–life balance. It is not enough for an organization to simply offer benefits— employees must feel safe and supported in using them, without fear of professional consequences. The companies that succeed in fostering balance are those that actively reinforce a culture where boundaries are respected, flexibility is normalized, and parents are seen as valuable assets rather than liabilities.

As we described earlier in this chapter, one of the most powerful ways to shape culture is through leadership. Employees take their cues from the top, and when senior leaders model sustainable work habits, they send a strong message throughout the organization. At Patagonia, for example, executives openly prioritize family commitments, with the CEO frequently stepping away for school events and personal time. This leadership behavior normalizes balance across all levels, making it clear that parental responsibilities are not just tolerated but fully integrated into the company's culture. The result? Patagonia consistently ranks among the top companies for working parents, with retention rates significantly above industry averages.

By contrast, companies that fail to align leadership behavior with stated policies create an environment of silent penalties.

Employees may technically be allowed to take parental leave, but if they see colleagues who take extended leave being passed over for promotions or left out of key projects, the message is clear: career growth and family responsibilities are at odds. This perception is particularly damaging for women, who are disproportionately impacted by the motherhood penalty. Without a cultural shift that explicitly values parents as professionals, these disparities persist, reinforcing outdated gender dynamics in the workplace.

For culture to truly support work–life boundaries, it must be embedded into everyday practices and norms. Central to this is redefining the language and narratives around parental leave and flexibility. Instead of framing parental leave as an "absence" or a "gap" in an employee's career, leading organizations are beginning to talk about it as a period of professional and personal growth. Bain & Company, a global consulting firm, recently introduced a parental leave reintegration program that highlights the leadership and time-management skills employees develop during their leave. By reframing the conversation, they shift the perception of leave, transforming it from a career setback to a natural and valuable phase of professional development.

Beyond leadership modeling and language shifts, culture is also shaped by the way teams and colleagues respond to boundaries. A company that claims to respect work–life balance but tolerates a culture where employees feel obligated to answer emails late at night or accept meetings outside of reasonable hours is not truly committed to balance. A culture is not just about policies—it is about day-to-day accountability and behavior.

One of the most successful case studies in cultural transformation comes from Spotify. Recognizing that many employees felt hesitant to use their generous parental leave policies, the company implemented a proactive "family-first" culture initiative. Instead of simply offering extended leave, they actively encouraged employees to take it by highlighting parental leave success stories, ensuring that those who took leave were promoted at the same rate as their peers, and training managers on how to support employees through transitions. Within three years, Spotify saw a 30 percent increase in parental leave uptake, a sharp decline in turnover among new parents, and an increase in gender diversity at leadership levels.

Culture, at its core, is not just stated values. It is a set of collective behaviors that reflect those values. When employees see their colleagues setting boundaries without negative repercussions, they feel empowered to do the same. When teams respect one another's off-hours and avoid rewarding overwork, they create an environment where balance is not just possible but expected.

For managers, shifting culture requires more than just approving requests for flexibility or parental leave—it requires actively reinforcing boundary setting as a norm. This means recognizing and celebrating employees who maintain healthy work–life integration, rather than only rewarding those who push themselves to the brink. It means fostering open conversations about workload and ensuring that those who take time for family are not subtly penalized in career opportunities. And most importantly, it means holding both leaders and peers accountable for creating an environment where employees do not have to choose between being a good parent and a successful professional.

At the end of the day, culture is what determines whether work–life boundaries are truly sustainable. It is what makes the difference between a policy that exists on paper and a reality where employees feel valued, respected, and empowered to thrive both at work and at home. And for companies looking to attract and retain top talent in an increasingly competitive market, getting this right is not optional—it is essential.

Conclusion: Boundaries as a Business Strategy

Workplaces thrive when employees are engaged, focused, and supported. Yet for too long, the professional world has treated parenthood as an obstacle to career success rather than a source of strength. The reality is that helping employees establish and maintain boundaries—both during parental leave and upon their return—is not just about doing the right thing; it is a strategic advantage for companies looking to attract, retain, and empower top talent.

When organizations fail to set clear boundaries, new parents are left struggling to navigate unrealistic expectations, often caught between the pressure to perform at work and the responsibilities pulling them home. The result is a workforce where burnout is common, disengagement is inevitable, and turnover is costly. But when companies take a proactive approach—ensuring that emotional, cultural, and time boundaries are not only supported but actively enforced—everyone benefits.

The future of work is not about demanding constant availability or forcing employees to choose between career success and family life. It is about creating environments where both are possible, where employees can contribute at a high level without sacrificing their personal well-being. And the organizations that recognize this will not only attract the best talent—they will keep it.

As businesses continue to evolve in an era of increasing demands for flexibility, inclusion, and sustainability, one truth remains clear: workplaces that support parents with strong, respected boundaries are workplaces that win. The companies that embrace this reality will not just survive in the modern business landscape—they will lead it.

Key Takeaways

- **Boundaries improve retention and performance.**
  Companies that actively support work–life boundaries see
  higher employee engagement, lower turnover, and stronger
  long-term commitment.
- **Leadership sets the tone.** If managers respect parental
  leave and flexible work, employees feel empowered to do
  the same without fear of career consequences.
- **Flexibility must be structured.** True flexibility is more
  than remote work—it requires clear policies, defined
  hours, and performance metrics based on impact, not
  hours worked.
- **The always-on culture is damaging.** Employees who feel
  pressured to be available at all times are less productive,
  more stressed, and more likely to leave.
- **Return-to-work programs boost retention.** Companies
  with structured reintegration plans retain more than 90
  percent of new parents, compared to only 76 percent in
  companies without such plans.
- **Culture matters more than policy.** Policies alone don't
  drive change—organizations must actively encourage
  employees to set boundaries and enforce them at every
  level.

Reflection

1. How can you ensure that your team members feel
   comfortable setting and maintaining work–life
   boundaries?
2. Have you ever hesitated to set boundaries at work? If so,
   what fears or pressures influenced that hesitation?
3. What implicit messages does your company leadership
   send about availability and commitment? How can you
   change those narratives?

4. What structured support systems (e.g., phased return-to-work programs, flexible scheduling) would improve work–life integration in your company?
5. How can teams hold each other accountable for respecting boundaries without relying solely on leadership to enforce them?

6 | REDEFINING IDENTITY AND PURPOSE

In the weeks following the arrival of a child, life takes on a rhythm that feels both familiar and entirely foreign. Days once marked by the predictability of work schedules and social commitments are now carved up by constantly changing feeding and sleeping schedules, endless laundry, and unpredictable needs. The new rhythm is exhausting, exhilarating, and profoundly disorienting. For most parents, this shift is not just logistical but deeply personal. Parenthood doesn't simply add new tasks to your to-do list, it transforms your sense of self. The role of parent doesn't neatly replace existing identities like professional, partner, or friend; instead, it layers itself atop them, creating a mosaic of competing priorities, emotions, and expectations.

Profound change clarifies so many things. While change is often stressful, even painful, it takes us through a process of examining and reexamining our lives, both from a long-term aspirational perspective and in the day-to-day and moment-to-moment decisions about how to allocate our energy and time. We are what we do, and balancing parenthood and career intensifies this process.

This chapter dives into the heart of this identity transformation. We explore how new parents navigate the profound shift in their roles, both at home and at work, and how this transition reshapes their values and sense of purpose. From the struggle to balance ambition with presence, to the opportunity to redefine success on your terms, we'll unpack the messy, beautiful process of becoming not just a parent, but a new and more resilient version of yourself.

Navigating the Shift in Identity

When Alex, an analyst at a fast-growing tech company, returned to work three weeks after the birth of his daughter Mia, he thought he had planned for everything. He'd carefully coordinated his leave, delegated projects, and even set up a home office to handle late-night emergencies. But what he hadn't anticipated was the internal conflict.

"Every decision felt loaded," Alex admitted. "If I stayed late to finish a project, I felt like I was missing precious moments at home. But if I left early, I worried my team thought I wasn't pulling my weight. I sort of felt like two people inhabiting the same body, with different priorities."

Alex's experience is strikingly common. New parents often find themselves caught between two worlds, each demanding their full attention. The workplace values productivity, ambition, and availability. Parenthood, on the other hand, calls for presence, patience, and emotional investment. Reconciling these demands requires not just practical adjustments but a fundamental shift in how parents perceive their own identity. It is not an either–or choice, but rather a both–and.

Parenthood doesn't erase who you were before; it adds layers to your identity. Sociologist Shelley Correll describes this phenomenon as "identity layering," a process where old roles and ambitions don't disappear but coexist with new ones, often creating tension and, eventually, growth.

Erica, a corporate attorney and first-time mother, had spent years cultivating her reputation as a rising star in her firm. After her son, Henry, was born, she felt an immediate shift. "I wasn't the go-to person for big cases anymore," she said. "And at home, I was too exhausted to be the mom I wanted to be. I felt like I was failing everywhere." It wasn't until a conversation with a mentor that Erica reframed her situation. "She told me success isn't about doing everything at 100 percent all the time," Erica shared. "It's about learning to prioritize and adapt."

For many parents, this process of adaptation involves re-defining what success means in both personal and professional contexts. It's not about replacing one identity with another but learning to embrace a more complex, multifaceted self.

Traditional measures of success—promotions, accolades, and packed schedules—often feel inadequate or even counter-productive in the context of new parenthood. Instead, parents must adopt a more fluid definition of success that aligns with their evolving priorities.

Consider Kia and Raj, software engineers who became parents to premature twins. Before their daughters were born, their lives were meticulously planned, from certifications to career milestones. But after months spent in the NICU with their twins, their definition of success changed. "Success was getting through the day," Kia said. "If I could attend one meeting and help my daughter smile, that was enough."

Kia and Raj's story underscores the importance of flexibility and perspective. For new parents, success might mean temporar-ily scaling back at work or celebrating small wins, like finishing a task or having a meaningful moment with their child. However, even with small successes, parents may start to feel like the new venture is overwhelming and fall victim to imposter syndrome.

Imposter Syndrome: The Struggle of Being Both Parent and Professional

Imposter syndrome is a feeling that many professionals are fa-miliar with, yet few talk about openly. It's that nagging thought that you're somehow not qualified for your role, that you've somehow "tricked" others into thinking you're capable, or that you're waiting for the day when your lack of knowledge or skills will be exposed. Many successful individuals—whether they are leaders, high performers, or those climbing the cor-porate ladder—have felt this sense of self-doubt at one point or another. It can affect anyone, no matter their experience, achievements, or qualifications. The more we grow in our careers, the higher we tend to set our standards, and with that expansion can come the overwhelming feeling that we're not living up to those expectations.

Interestingly, this feeling of being an imposter can have striking parallels to the experience of becoming a new parent. When parents first step into their new role, they often feel woefully unprepared. Despite all the books they've read, advice they've listened to, and prenatal classes they've attended, many parents feel an overwhelming sense of self-doubt the moment their baby is placed in their arms. The transition into parenthood can make them question their readiness, their ability to provide the care their child needs, and whether they are capable of living up to the expectations placed upon them. Much like a professional experiencing imposter syndrome, a new parent may wonder: *Am I really ready for this?*

This sense of being unqualified or unprepared doesn't come from a lack of skill but from the unfamiliarity and complexity of the new role. Just as a professional may feel out of place when transitioning to a higher-level position or facing a new project, a new parent may feel unprepared when facing the complexities of child-rearing, no matter how much research they've done. The challenge is not a lack of ability, but the realization that parenthood is a deeply personal, ongoing learning process, filled with unpredictable challenges and milestones.

The comparison between imposter syndrome and new parenthood is important because it illustrates that feelings of inadequacy are often part of the growth process. Both roles—parent and professional—are dynamic and ever changing. Professionals sometimes feel like imposters in new, unfamiliar projects or roles because they are navigating unknown territory and learning as they go. Similarly, new parents are thrust into a role with no clear road map, and the learning curve can feel steep, especially in the face of sleepless nights, emotional highs and lows, and the sheer magnitude of responsibility.

However, just as professionals overcome imposter syndrome through experience, support, and reflection on their strengths, new parents gradually come to realize that their feelings of inadequacy are part of the normal, inevitable process of growth. With time, they gain confidence in their parenting skills, just as professionals build confidence in their abilities at work. They learn to trust their instincts, ask for help when they need it, and take pride in the small wins—whether it's comforting a crying baby or successfully leading a project.

Ultimately, both parenthood and professional growth require the same recognition: *You don't need to have all the answers, but you do need to be willing to learn.* Imposter syndrome and the feeling of being unprepared as a new parent are not signs of failure, but rather indicators that you are stepping outside your comfort zone. The key is to embrace the learning process, be kind to yourself, and acknowledge that feeling unsure is part of becoming who you are or want to be, both as a professional and a parent. Instead of being afraid to acknowledge your doubts, embrace the vulnerability.

Embracing Vulnerability and Setting Boundaries During Parental Leave

Parental leave brings a profound sense of vulnerability, especially for professionals accustomed to control and high achievement. The early stages of parenthood often upend routines, priorities, and self-perception, making it critical to establish boundaries that protect emotional and mental well-being. For many, the hardest part is asking for what they need—stepping back, slowing down, or saying no. But setting boundaries during this time isn't a retreat from responsibility; it's a strategic act of self-care that allows new parents to recover, recalibrate, and return with clarity. Vulnerability and boundaries go hand in hand, and together they create the conditions for sustainable growth. As we'll explore further in the chapter on returnship, a healthy reintegration begins here—with honest conversations, clear limits, and the recognition that thriving at home and at work starts with respecting the space in between.

Changing Priorities and the Struggle to Balance Them

The idea of balance has become something of a myth in modern parenting. Everyone talks about achieving it, but few agree on what it looks like, and even fewer feel like they've attained it. Parenthood shifts the axis of your life. Goals that once seemed clear and linear—hitting deadlines, achieving promotions, sticking to a fitness plan—suddenly compete with new priorities like feeding schedules, pediatric appointments, and the bare minimum of sleep. It's not that one set of responsibilities is more important than the other; it's that both feel urgent and nonnegotiable.

This internal tug-of-war is often amplified by external pressures. Colleagues, supervisors, and even well-meaning friends may unintentionally reinforce the idea that balancing work and parenting is a matter of personal discipline or organization, rather than acknowledging that it requires systemic support and a willingness to redefine success.

For many new parents, the first step in navigating these shifting priorities is to acknowledge that the scales will rarely, if ever, feel perfectly balanced. Instead of aiming for equilibrium, it's more realistic—and kinder—to focus on intentionality. What truly matters in this moment? What can wait? Parenthood narrows the aperture of your life. Because doing everything isn't possible, choices have to be made and priorities emerge. While this can feel like a loss, it is in many ways a gain because one's energy can be channeled into what is truly important and nurturing for oneself and others. However, this pivot requires enough thoughtfulness and intention to see clearly the choices at hand. These choices are at the heart of how parenthood can redefine identity and clarify purpose.

Take Justin, a product manager and new father, as an example. Before the birth of his son, Justin prided himself on his 5 a.m.

workouts, meticulous project planning, and after-hours networking. "I had a system, and it worked," he said. "But after Liam was born, the system fell apart." Justin's workouts disappeared, his inbox overflowed, and his evenings were spent soothing a colicky baby.

It wasn't until Justin sat down with his wife to reassess their shared priorities that things began to shift. They created a list of nonnegotiables—things they both needed to feel sane and supported—and then delegated or let go of everything else. For Justin, this meant dropping his early-morning workouts in favor of quick afternoon runs, scaling back on nonessential work meetings, and hiring a cleaning service to reduce household stress.

The lesson here is simple but profound: priorities aren't static. They evolve, sometimes daily, based on your family's needs, your work demands, and your own mental and physical well-being. The challenge lies in being flexible enough to adjust without feeling like you're losing yourself in the process.

The Cognitive Dissonance Between Personal Perspectives and Societal Messages

Society often sends mixed messages about what new parents should strive for. On one hand, there's the expectation to fully immerse yourself in parenting, cherishing every milestone and moment. On the other hand, there's the relentless pressure to remain professionally ambitious, fit, and socially active. Most people become parents during the time of life when professional identity is most important, and when the need to earn and save is most crucial. This dials up the stress.

The cultural narrative of "having it all" is not only unrealistic but harmful. It sets parents up for failure by suggesting that any compromise—whether skipping a networking event to attend a school play or choosing formula over breastfeeding—is a sign of inadequacy. While any parent can feel squeezed by these sorts of societal expectations, the pressure is often worse for women.

Marissa, a financial analyst and mother of twins, described her experience of trying to live up to conflicting expectations. "I felt like I was always apologizing," she said. "To my boss for leaving early, to my kids for not being fully present, and even to myself for not being the kind of mom or professional I thought I should be." Research supports Marissa's feelings. A theme in many studies on working parents found that working parents often experience "role conflict," where the demands of one domain (e.g., work) directly interfere with their ability to meet the expectations of another (e.g., parenting). This conflict is especially pronounced for women, who are more likely to shoulder the dual burdens of professional and household responsibilities, but men are not immune.

One way to counter this narrative is to redefine what "all" means. For some parents, it might mean leaning into their careers during certain seasons of life while scaling back during others. For others, it might involve rejecting societal expectations altogether and focusing on what feels authentic and sustainable for their family. The stresses of parenthood can provide the impetus to decide for yourself, and in this way to redefine your identity.

Strategies for Managing the Struggle

While there's no one-size-fits-all solution to balancing changing priorities, there are strategies that can help. These strategies don't eliminate the challenges but offer a framework for navigating them with more clarity and intention.

- **Build a strong support network.** Parenthood is not a solo endeavor. Whether it's a partner, family member, friend, or coworker, having people you can lean on makes a world of difference. Research from the American Psychological Association (APA) shows that social support is a critical factor in mitigating stress and maintaining mental health, particularly during major life transitions.[1]

For single mother Clara, her support network was her workplace. After openly sharing her struggles with her supervisor, Clara was paired with a mentor who had navigated similar challenges. "Just knowing someone else had been through it—and come out stronger—was incredibly reassuring," she said.

- **Embrace imperfection.** The pursuit of perfection is one of the biggest sources of stress for new parents. Accepting that some things will fall by the wayside—or that you may not excel in every area all the time—can be liberating.

  When Daniel, a graphic designer, accidentally missed his daughter's first pediatric appointment because of a work deadline, he felt crushed. But instead of spiraling into guilt, he used the moment as a learning opportunity. "I realized I was trying to do too much," he said. "So, I sat down with my wife, and we created a shared calendar to avoid mix-ups in the future."

- **Communicate transparently.** Open communication with colleagues, supervisors, and even clients is essential for managing expectations. Many parents fear being perceived as less committed to their jobs, but transparency can foster understanding and lead to solutions that benefit everyone.

  Take Ruth, an attorney who negotiated a reduced caseload during her son's first six months. "It wasn't easy to ask," she admitted. "But my firm was surprisingly supportive, and it allowed me to be more present at home without sacrificing the quality of my work."

Ultimately, balancing changing priorities isn't about achieving a perfect division of time or energy. It's about learning to adapt, making intentional choices, and celebrating small wins along the way.

Parenthood is, by nature, a series of trade-offs. The key is to ensure those trade-offs align with your values and priorities. When you give yourself permission to let go of unrealistic expectations and embrace the messiness, you create space for what truly matters: connection, growth, and a life that feels meaningful on your terms.

The Opportunity to Reassess Values

The first few months of life with a newborn are often described as a blur. Days and nights lose definition, and the hours are long but the months are short. Amidst the chaos, there exists a rare opportunity—a chance to pause, reflect, and fundamentally reassess what matters most. These months are a time when the walls of routine collapse, and the scaffolding of your priorities becomes exposed, forcing a profound reevaluation of what holds meaning in your life.

Identity and values exist and evolve together. For many, parenthood is a mirror that reflects both who we are and who we aspire to be. Philosopher Søren Kierkegaard once wrote, "Life must be understood backwards; but . . . it must be lived forwards." New parents often live out this paradox, forced to reckon with past decisions while imagining the kind of future they want to create for their child and themselves. This tension between past and future leads parents to reexamine and reshape their values, even as their identities solidify and change.

Consider the story of Lydia and Adam, a dual-career couple in their early thirties. Before their son, Noah, was born, their lives were finely tuned to professional ambition. Adam, a lawyer, worked twelve-hour days, while Lydia, a marketing director, was equally consumed by quarterly targets and client demands. Their careers defined them. But when Noah arrived six weeks early, their meticulously planned lives unraveled. Noah's unexpected early birth brought weeks of NICU visits, long nights, and an abrupt confrontation with their priorities.

In the quiet hours spent beside Noah's incubator, Lydia found herself questioning the relentless pace she had once celebrated. Did career accolades matter more than moments with her son? Meanwhile, Adam began to wrestle with guilt—his absence from home during Lydia's pregnancy now felt like a gaping void he couldn't undo. As they sat together, exhausted but deeply present, they began to outline what they wanted their life to look like moving forward. Time with family took precedence over work, and they committed to carving out shared responsibilities that reflected their evolving values. They also had a clearer sense of how they wanted to grow their careers and how their chosen work paths could support their new lives.

Such reassessment is not uncommon during the early months of parenthood. When stripped of the distractions of daily life, parents often uncover a clarity that is difficult to access during normal routines. This clarity, however, doesn't come easily. It often arises from tension—between what we believe we value and how we spend our time. Fred, an older father, expressed that he valued physical health so that he could be vibrant and healthy and participate in sports with his children as they grew into teenagers. However, he was spending significant time on social media sites, more than he was acknowledging. Once the kids were born, this tension emerged and he was able to make clearer choices about the highest values-based use of his time. When they establish clarity in their personal lives, parents are able to translate that clarity to their professional ambitions and create a stronger alignment.

The philosopher Simone Weil wrote extensively about attention as a moral act. "Attention," she argued, "is the rarest and purest form of generosity." Parenthood forces attention in its purest form. You are required to focus on the immediate needs of your child, but in doing so, you also can begin to pay attention to yourself. What truly fulfills you? What drains you? What has merely been noise in your life up until now?

This period of reflection aligns closely with the concept of eudaimonia, or "flourishing," as described in Aristotelian ethics. Aristotle argued that a flourishing life is one lived in alignment with one's core virtues and values. Yet, for many of us, these values remain unarticulated, buried beneath the demands of work, relationships, and social expectations. Parenthood, with its raw and demanding nature, brings these values to the forefront, offering a chance to recalibrate.

For example, Karen, a first-time mother and midlevel manager, entered parental leave without expecting to return to her career, which she found to be dull. But during her three months at home with her daughter, she began to write short stories to read for bedtime. This act rekindled her love for creative writing, a passion she had abandoned years earlier. Slowly, she began to see how her career in corporate communications could evolve to make space for this dormant part of herself. By the time her leave ended, she was excited to restart her career. Karen had a clearer vision of how to integrate her professional and personal aspirations.

These moments of reassessment are not limited to career or hobbies. They extend to relationships, lifestyle choices, and even spiritual practices. For many, the early months of parenthood are a time to ask: Am I living a life aligned with who I want to be?

Values in Practice

Reassessing values is one thing; living them out is another. The transition back to work, the mounting financial pressures of childcare, and the sheer exhaustion of new parenthood can make it difficult to translate newfound clarity into action. This is where intentionality becomes crucial.

Take, for instance, Tom and Hugo, a couple who decided during Hugo's leave that they wanted to prioritize family dinners as a nonnegotiable ritual. For years, Tom's unpredictable work schedule as a software engineer had made such routines impossible. Hugo worked from home and often ate dinner alone or out with friends. But after months of evening feedings and bonding with their daughter, they realized how much they valued that shared time. When Tom returned to work, he negotiated flexible hours with his manager, ensuring he could be home by six o'clock most nights. This small but significant adjustment allowed them to live out their commitment to family connection. The new ritual strengthened their relationships and reduced their overall work–life tension.

The process of reassessment also often leads to difficult but necessary choices. For some parents, it might mean stepping back from leadership roles or turning down promotions that conflict with their newly clarified priorities. For others, it might mean doubling down on professional ambitions but in a way that feels more intentional and aligned with long-term goals.

In the corporate world, there is increasing recognition of the importance of this kind of values-based decision making. Some companies now offer structured programs to help employees navigate life transitions, including parenthood. These programs often include coaching sessions or workshops that encourage employees to articulate their values and set intentions for how they want to balance work and family life. Several of the interviewees for this book told us that their employers had recently made coaching available for new parents, and in some cases for managers of new parents. When their managers received coaching, these new parents felt more supported.

Finally, it's important to acknowledge that reassessing values doesn't happen in isolation. It is deeply influenced by the support systems—or lack thereof—surrounding new parents. Partners, family members, friends, and even workplaces play a crucial role in creating the space and time for this reflection to occur.

For single parents or those without robust support networks, this process can feel overwhelming. But even in these cases, small acts of self-compassion and deliberate boundary setting can make a significant difference. Seeking out community—whether through parenting groups, online forums, or even therapy—can provide the perspective and encouragement they need to navigate this complex period.

Ultimately, the values that emerge during these early months often set the tone for years to come. They influence how parents approach their careers, relationships, and parenting styles. And while the specifics may evolve as children grow and life circumstances change, the act of reassessment itself becomes a lifelong practice.

In many ways, this period serves as a reminder of the transient but transformative nature of parenthood. It is a season that strips away pretenses, exposes vulnerabilities, and offers a rare window into what truly matters. The challenge, of course, is to carry those insights forward—to allow the clarity gained during sleepless nights and quiet moments of reflection to shape the decisions that follow. Parents may be consciously assessing and realigning their values even as they are unknowingly strengthening a trait that will support their new intentions in the long term: resilience.

Conclusion: Embracing the Transformation

Parenthood is a profound transformation, one that challenges, reshapes, and ultimately refines identity and purpose. The transition into this new role brings moments of self-doubt, imposter syndrome, and the weight of competing priorities, yet it also presents an unparalleled opportunity for growth. The struggles of balancing career and caregiving are real, but rather than diminishing professional capabilities, parenthood enhances them. It sharpens skills like adaptability, resilience, emotional intelligence, and prioritization, attributes that are as valuable in the workplace as they are in raising a child.

The stories shared in this chapter illustrate that identity is not lost in parenthood; it is expanded. Success is no longer measured solely by professional achievements but by the ability to integrate evolving priorities with intention and authenticity. Parenthood demands a reassessment of values, and through this process, many discover a clearer sense of purpose, both at home and at work.

This journey is not about achieving perfect balance but about making intentional choices that align with what truly matters. It requires vulnerability, boundary setting, and a willingness to redefine expectations—not just for oneself, but within workplaces and societal structures. As more organizations recognize the value parents bring to the workforce, there is hope for a cultural shift that posits career and caregiving as being in harmony rather than in opposition.

Ultimately, the transition into parenthood is one of life's most demanding yet rewarding evolutions. It offers the chance to not only raise a child but also to grow into a more resilient, intentional, and purpose-driven version of oneself. Rather than resisting the change, embracing the transformation allows parents to step into their new identities with confidence, clarity, and a renewed sense of what truly matters.

Key Takeaways

- **Support systems are essential.** Partners, family, friends, and professionals play a critical role in lightening the burden and fostering resilience.
- **Stress can foster growth.** With the right balance, manageable stress enhances problem solving and emotional regulation, contributing to long-term coping skills.
- **Perspective matters.** Reframing challenges as meaningful acts of love can transform overwhelming moments into opportunities for connection and growth.
- **Small steps build stability.** Micro-routines, rest, self-care, and celebrating small successes provide essential anchors during chaotic times.

Reflection

1. If you were a new parent with an opportunity for career advancement that required a lot more work and/or travel, what factors would you consider in making your decision?
2. How might workplace policies (such as flexible schedules, project structuring, or return-to-work programs) provide systemic support for employees looking to embrace new opportunities and maintain their career trajectory without burning out?
3. How should companies train managers to better support employees navigating major life transitions like parenthood?
4. Have you ever experienced a situation where your personal priorities and professional expectations felt misaligned? How did you handle it?

7 | THE DEVELOPMENTAL JOURNEY

When a working professional becomes a parent, the assumption is often that their focus will shift away from career ambitions. This is particularly true for women but, as we've discussed, it can also be true for men who take a less traditional path in balancing career and family. Colleagues and managers may quietly expect a decline in performance, a scaling back of responsibilities, or even an eventual exit from leadership tracks. The unspoken belief is that parenthood and professional growth exist in tension rather than in harmony.

But what if the opposite were true?

What if parenthood didn't hinder career progression, but rather enhanced it?

The reality is that parenthood is one of the most effective leadership development programs available—only, it doesn't come with a formal certificate or an executive training badge. It is a high-stakes, immersive crash course in decision making, crisis management, negotiation, emotional intelligence, and resilience. It teaches professionals how to operate under pressure, balance competing priorities, and lead with both authority and empathy.

And yet, too often, these skills are undervalued or overlooked in the corporate world. Managers may see new parents as distracted, less available, or unable to handle high-stakes projects. Meanwhile, working parents themselves may not realize how much their personal growth translates to professional excellence.

This chapter aims to shift that perspective.

Through research, case studies, and real-life examples, we'll explore how parenthood sharpens the very competencies that make great leaders. We'll examine how navigating a toddler's tantrum strengthens crisis management skills, how juggling a newborn's needs refines prioritization, and how responding to a child's anxieties builds emotional intelligence that translates seamlessly into managing teams.

For corporate managers, this chapter provides a new framework for recognizing, developing, and leveraging the leadership potential of working parents. For parents, it offers a reframing of their own experiences, helping them see how the challenges of raising children are not detours from their professional growth but accelerators of it.

Parenthood isn't a roadblock. It's a proving ground.

Let's explore how.

The Overlapping Skill Sets of Parenting and Leadership

At first glance, the daily responsibilities of a parent—diaper changes, school drop-offs, bedtime routines—might seem to have little in common with the demands of corporate leadership. But beneath these surface-level tasks lies a deeper reality: parenting is an ongoing exercise in decision making, strategic thinking, and emotional intelligence, the very skills that define effective leadership.

In fact, the skills that parents develop out of necessity mirror those required to manage teams, navigate crises, and drive business success. Consider the following parallels:

Parenting Skill	Corporate Leadership Equivalent
Managing tantrums and emotional outbursts	Handling workplace conflicts and negotiations
Prioritizing needs of multiple children	Managing competing business priorities
Making decisions with limited information	Leading through uncertainty
Teaching and guiding children	Coaching and mentoring employees
Staying composed under stress	Managing crises and maintaining executive presence
Encouraging resilience and independence	Developing strong, self-sufficient teams

A growing body of research supports the idea that parenthood enhances executive skills. Studies have shown that parents, particularly mothers returning to the workforce, experience increased efficiency, improved multitasking, and stronger problem-solving capabilities. In our interview research, time and time again, parents have noted how they are far more adept at multitasking and managing their time effectively. Despite the evidence, many corporate cultures still operate under the assumption that parenthood is a liability rather than an asset. The reality is that a parent returning from leave has not fallen behind; they have, in many ways, been through an intensive leadership-training experience that companies would do well to recognize and harness.

The Managerial Perspective: Rethinking Leadership Potential

For corporate managers, the idea that parenting can be an informal yet intense leadership boot camp raises an important question: Is the organization overlooking high-potential talent simply because an employee's leadership training occurred outside the corporate headquarters?

When assessing employees for leadership roles, managers often look for individuals who demonstrate resilience, strategic decision making, and strong interpersonal skills. These qualities are developed through experience, and few experiences cultivate them as rapidly or intensively as parenthood.

If companies genuinely want to build strong, adaptable leaders, they need to shift their perspective. Instead of seeing working parents as employees with distractions, they should recognize them as professionals who have gained real-world leadership experience.

This shift in thinking is essential, not only to support working parents but to strengthen organizations as a whole. In the following sections, we take a deeper dive into how parenthood fosters key leadership competencies, from crisis management to emotional intelligence, and explore actionable ways for managers to leverage this talent within their teams.

Crisis Management and Decision Making Under Pressure

Crisis management is a defining skill for any leader. In high-stakes business environments, leaders must remain calm under pressure, assess risks quickly, and make critical decisions, often with incomplete information. These same skills are sharpened daily in parenthood, where the unexpected is the norm.

Parenting as a Crash Course in Crisis Management

Ask any parent about their experience with a sudden fever at 2 a.m., a toddler's public meltdown, or an unexpected childcare cancellation before an important work meeting, and you'll get a master class in crisis response. Parenthood forces individuals to:

- **Assess situations rapidly.** Is this an emergency or something that can wait?
- **Prioritize immediate action.** What needs to be addressed first, and what can be deferred?
- **Manage emotions under pressure.** How can I de-escalate this situation while maintaining control?

- **Adapt when plans fail.** What's the backup solution when the original plan falls apart?

These are the very same competencies that define effective business leaders. A corporate executive facing a product failure, a public relations crisis, or a sudden market downturn must also act swiftly, prioritize responses, and manage emotions, both their own and those of their teams.

From the Homefront to the Boardroom

Consider Charles, a project manager who was on paternity leave when a major crisis hit his company. While caring for his newborn, he was unexpectedly called to help manage a critical situation, one that required high-stakes decision making. Having already spent weeks in a sleep-deprived state, making rapid decisions to care for his newborn while supporting his partner, Charles found that he was able to assess the crisis with a surprising level of clarity. His experience as a new parent had trained him to compartmentalize stress, focus on the most urgent issues, and delegate where needed, all essential crisis leadership skills.

His story is far from unique. Parents, by necessity, develop the ability to remain composed in moments of unpredictability. Their capacity to navigate chaos and make sound decisions while under pressure is a direct advantage in the workplace.

What Corporate Leaders Can Learn from Parents

For managers looking to identify and promote strong leaders, crisis response is a critical metric. Yet, companies often rely on traditional indicators—such as past project performance or technical expertise—without fully recognizing how personal experiences shape leadership capabilities.

Here's how corporate leaders can rethink crisis leadership potential:

- **Look beyond formal leadership experience.** An employee who has managed a chaotic household with young children likely has better crisis-management skills than someone who has never had to navigate high-pressure situations outside of work.

- **Recognize resilience and adaptability.** Parents develop a heightened ability to pivot when circumstances change, a key asset in today's fast-moving business landscape.
- **Provide leadership opportunities that leverage these strengths.** Managers should consider placing working parents in roles that require decision making under uncertainty, such as managing high-profile client accounts or leading urgent projects.

By reframing parenthood as a proving ground for crisis leadership, companies can tap into a talent pool that is often undervalued. Parenthood isn't just about surviving chaos—it's about learning to lead through it.

Prioritization, Delegation, and Strategic Thinking

In both parenting and corporate leadership, the ability to prioritize effectively can mean the difference between success and chaos. With an ever-growing list of demands, both parents and executives must decide what gets immediate attention, what can be delegated, and what can wait. Parenthood is an intensive, real-world training ground for mastering these skills.

Parenting as a Masterclass in Prioritization

From the moment a baby is born, parents become expert prioritizers. They quickly learn to distinguish between what is urgent—feeding a hungry newborn, addressing a medical issue—and what can be postponed—folding laundry or responding to noncritical emails. The ability to focus on high-impact actions while tuning out distractions is a hallmark of strong leadership.

Consider the mental triage a parent performs daily:

- What must happen right now? (The baby is crying, and a bottle needs to be warmed.)
- What is important but not urgent? (Registering for preschool in six months is on the to-do list but not at the top.)
- What is noise and can be ignored? (That perfect Pinterest-worthy birthday party can wait.)

This mirrors the decisions that corporate leaders make every day, whether they're managing a product launch, handling competing deadlines, or leading a team through a major transition. Effective leaders know that success isn't about doing everything at once; it's about doing the right things at the right time.

Delegation: Learning to Let Go

Many first-time parents struggle with delegation, wanting to handle every detail themselves. But as any experienced parent knows, trying to do it all alone is a fast track to burnout. Parenthood teaches a valuable leadership lesson: trusting others to take on responsibility is not just helpful—it's necessary.

The ability to delegate effectively translates directly to the workplace. Leaders who struggle to hand off tasks often find themselves overwhelmed, while those who empower their teams to take ownership of projects create a more efficient and engaged workforce. Parents—having already learned the art of enlisting help from partners, family members, and caregivers—often bring a strong sense of collaboration and team building to their professional roles.

However, like every good leader who delegates in ways that create learning and success, a parent only delegates tasks that can be done safely and effectively. A parent who wants help with their children will set up close friends and family members for success, so they will help again! Good delegation is more than task assignment.

Take, for example, a marketing director who recently became a father. Before parenthood, he was known for micromanaging projects, often feeling the need to review every detail himself. After becoming a parent, he realized the value of delegation, not just at home but also at work. He began trusting his team more, allowing them to take the lead on key initiatives, which not only reduced his stress but also improved overall team performance.

Strategic Thinking: Making the Most of Limited Time

Parenthood forces efficiency. Time becomes a scarce resource, and parents become acutely aware of how to maximize productivity within tight constraints. This often leads to enhanced strategic thinking, an invaluable skill in corporate leadership.

A working parent managing a packed schedule learns to ask:

- What will yield the greatest return on investment?
- Where should I allocate my limited time and energy?
- Which meetings, tasks, or projects are truly essential, and which can be streamlined or eliminated?

This is the same mindset that high-level executives use when making strategic business decisions. The best leaders know how to focus on high-impact activities while minimizing inefficiencies, an approach that parents practice every single day.

Emotional Intelligence and People Management

Great leaders don't just manage tasks; they manage people. The ability to understand, empathize with, and effectively communicate with others is what separates competent managers from truly exceptional leaders. While emotional intelligence (EQ) can be developed in many ways, few experiences hone it as rapidly and intensely as parenthood.

Parenting as an Emotional Intelligence Boot Camp

Raising children requires a high level of emotional awareness. Parents must anticipate their child's needs, manage emotional outbursts, and provide guidance in ways that foster trust and cooperation. Whether they are calming a frustrated toddler, mediating sibling disputes, or helping a teenager navigate anxiety, parents engage daily in emotional regulation, conflict resolution, and motivational leadership, all of which are essential qualities in effective corporate management.

The key dimensions of emotional intelligence—self-awareness, self-regulation, empathy, social skills, and motivation—are constantly in play for parents.

Emotional Intelligence Skill	Parenting Example	Corporate Leadership Parallel
Self-Awareness	Recognizing personal frustration when a child refuses to listen and adjusting reactions accordingly	Understanding personal triggers in workplace conflicts and managing responses effectively
Self-Regulation	Staying calm and patient during a child's meltdown instead of reacting emotionally	Remaining composed in high-pressure situations, such as a tense vendor or client negotiation
Empathy	Understanding why a child is acting out (tired, hungry, overwhelmed) and responding accordingly	Recognizing an employee's frustration or disengagement and addressing the root cause rather than just the symptoms
Social Skills	Teaching children how to communicate their feelings and resolve conflicts with others	Guiding teams through interpersonal challenges, fostering collaboration and productive communication
Motivation	Encouraging children to persist through difficulties, such as learning to ride a bike or studying for a test	Inspiring employees to stay engaged and work through challenges toward long-term success

How Parenthood Enhances Leadership in People Management

Consider Gil, a customer care center manager who found that parenthood deepened his ability to manage both employees and customers. Before having children, he viewed customer complaints as transactional problems to be solved. After becoming a father, he found himself approaching difficult customers with more patience and understanding, skills he had developed while navigating his own child's emotions. Instead of reacting defensively to frustrated customers, he began to de-escalate conflicts with empathy, which ultimately led to better customer satisfaction scores.

His approach to managing employees also changed. He became more attuned to his team's stress levels and learned to motivate different personalities in ways that resonated with them. Just as he recognized that one of his children needed structured guidance while the other thrived with autonomy, he understood that a personalized approach could be applied to his team, resulting in increased morale and performance.

These comparisons are not intended to imply that adult employees can be treated as a parent treats a child. They instead illustrate how the skills likely developed and employed by new parents are particularly relevant to leadership in general, and represent a resource to their employers.

It is also important to note that all new parents do not automatically acquire the leadership skills we are describing in this chapter. However, our interviews and broader research make a strong case that new parents are more likely to develop these skills, and that employers often don't give credence to the possibility (or probability) that new parents may be experiencing important skill development that their employer can seek to understand, support, and deploy in a way that helps the company.

Why Emotional Intelligence Is a Competitive Advantage

In today's corporate world, emotional intelligence is increasingly recognized as a critical leadership skill. Studies have shown that leaders with a high EQ are more successful at managing teams, reducing workplace conflicts, and improving overall organizational performance. In fact, a study by TalentSmartEQ found that 90 percent of top performers score high in emotional intelligence, while only 20 percent of low performers do.[1]

Three Ways Managers Can Leverage EQ in Working Parents

Identify parents as emotionally intelligent leaders. Recognize that their experience managing emotions and conflicts at home translates directly into workplace leadership.
Leverage parents' strengths in people management. Assign working parents to mentorship roles or positions that require strong interpersonal skills.
Redefine leadership potential beyond technical expertise. Instead of only promoting employees with the best technical skills, look for those who exhibit high emotional intelligence, often found in working parents.

By shifting the corporate mindset to recognize parenthood as a training ground for emotional intelligence, organizations can tap into a deeper, more dynamic pool of leadership talent.

Resilience and Adaptability

Parenthood doesn't just enhance cognitive and tactical skills—it deepens emotional endurance. The daily reality of raising a child requires showing up with steadiness, patience, and presence, even when circumstances are unclear or changing. Over time, this practice cultivates a kind of psychological durability: the ability to stay grounded, flexible, and effective under pressure. It's resilience not as a buzzword, but as lived experience.

Importantly, this kind of resilience isn't about pushing through at all costs. It's about learning to recalibrate—how to reframe setbacks, adapt plans in real time, and lead through ambiguity. Parents often report a shift in their relationship to uncertainty and control. Rather than resisting change, they become more adept at moving with it—making them valuable assets in environments that demand agility and emotional steadiness.

This growth often extends beyond the personal sphere. At work, these same individuals become better equipped to manage teams, navigate conflict, and support others through challenge. They are more attuned to nuance, more skilled at staying composed in the face of disruption, and more comfortable making imperfect decisions with care and clarity.

Organizations often list resilience and adaptability as top leadership competencies. What they may overlook is that these qualities are already present in many of their employees who are parents—not in spite of parenting, but because of it. The opportunity lies in recognizing, valuing, and leveraging that growth.

Communication, Negotiation, and Influence

Effective leaders aren't just problem solvers; they are skilled communicators and negotiators. They know how to persuade, de-escalate conflicts, and influence outcomes while maintaining strong relationships. These are precisely the skills that parents develop daily, whether convincing a stubborn toddler to put on shoes, mediating sibling disputes, or explaining complex concepts to a curious child.

Parenting as a Crash Course in Negotiation

Ask any parent, and they'll tell you: children are natural negotiators. Whether they are bargaining for five more minutes of playtime or pushing for a later bedtime, kids instinctively test boundaries and try to influence outcomes. Parents quickly learn that successful negotiation is not about winning every battle but about finding mutual solutions, setting clear expectations, and maintaining trust, all essential leadership skills.

A strong negotiator must:

- **Understand motivations and interests.** What does the other party truly want, and how can you align it with your goals? (For example, a parent offers "two more bedtime stories" instead of "five more minutes" to create a win–win.)
- **Remain calm and strategic.** Parents learn to control their emotions and avoid power struggles, just as corporate leaders must do in high-stakes negotiations.
- **Be persuasive without being authoritarian.** The best parents guide children toward good decisions rather than forcing compliance, similar to the way the best managers gain buy-in rather than imposing directives.

How Parenthood Sharpens Workplace Communication

Effective leadership hinges on the ability to communicate clearly, inspire confidence, and adjust messaging based on the audience. Parents develop these skills through everyday interactions, learning how to simplify complex ideas, listen actively, and choose words that resonate.

Consider a parent explaining to a skeptical child why eating vegetables is important. If they rely on logic alone ("Vegetables have vitamins"), they may fail. But if they adjust their communication strategy—perhaps by framing it as an exciting challenge or making it more engaging ("These carrots give you superhero vision!")—they are more likely to succeed.

In the workplace, the same principle applies. A manager explaining a strategic shift to employees needs to frame the message in a way that resonates, addresses concerns, and builds enthusiasm. Working parents, having honed this skill at home, often bring a higher level of adaptability and audience awareness to their workplace communication.

Why Communication and Negotiation Skills Are Essential for Leadership

In today's corporate world, leaders must navigate complex interpersonal dynamics, whether it's securing buy-in from stakeholders, resolving conflicts within teams, or influencing organizational change. Parents bring an advanced ability to assess situations, adapt communication styles, and negotiate effectively, often making them some of the strongest relationship builders in the workplace.

Three Ways Corporate Managers Can Leverage Parents' Strengths

Look for strong communicators among working parents. Their ability to explain, influence, and negotiate has been refined through daily real-world practice.
Assign them to negotiation-heavy roles. Working parents often excel in sales, client management, and leadership positions that require emotional intelligence and persuasion.
Leverage their conflict resolution skills. Encourage working parents to mentor younger employees or take on team leadership roles where communication is key.

By reframing parenting as a communication and negotiation training ground, companies can unlock the leadership potential of employees who have already mastered these critical skills.

Rethinking Career Trajectories for Parents

For too long, the corporate world has viewed parenthood as a career detour, an interruption to professional growth rather than an accelerator of leadership skills. This outdated perspective not only limits opportunities for working parents but also deprives organizations of a highly skilled, resilient, and adaptable talent pool.

It's time for a paradigm shift: instead of seeing working parents as employees with added constraints, companies should recognize them as professionals who have enhanced their leadership abilities through real-world experience.

Why Companies Need to Rethink Leadership Pipelines

The corporate world invests billions in leadership development programs, yet many organizations overlook a critical source of leadership talent: working parents. Companies that recognize parenthood as a leadership accelerator will gain a competitive edge in talent retention, employee engagement, and overall performance.

Here's how companies can rethink their approach:

1. **Redefine leadership readiness.** Instead of focusing solely on traditional corporate experiences, recognize the leadership skills developed through parenthood.
2. **Reevaluate career progression paths.** Ensure that parental leave and flexible schedules do not slow down promotions for employees who have demonstrated strong leadership abilities.
3. **Create return-to-work programs with leadership opportunities.** Provide pathways for parents returning to work to step into leadership roles that leverage their enhanced skills.
4. **Train managers to recognize the value of parenthood-driven leadership growth.** Help leaders understand how parenthood enhances key competencies and ensure that performance evaluations reflect these strengths.

For Working Parents: Owning Your Leadership Growth

While companies must evolve, working parents can also take ownership of their professional growth by recognizing and articulating the skills they've gained through parenthood.

• **Translate parenting experiences into business language.** Instead of saying, "I became great at multitasking as a parent," say, "I developed strong prioritization and crisis-management skills, allowing me to lead effectively under pressure."

• **Advocate for your value.** If you've strengthened your ability to manage teams, negotiate, or handle crises during parenthood, highlight these skills in performance reviews and leadership discussions.

• **Challenge outdated assumptions.** If an opportunity is presented to a nonparent colleague instead of you, based on the assumption that you're "too busy," be proactive in expressing your interest and readiness.

The Corporate Call to Action

The message is clear: parenthood is not a career setback; it's a leadership accelerator. Organizations that recognize and leverage this reality will retain top talent, build stronger leaders, and create a more innovative, resilient workforce.

By shifting corporate mindsets and breaking outdated biases, companies can unlock one of the most underappreciated sources of leadership talent: the working parent.

Conclusion: Parenthood as a Leadership Accelerator

For decades, the corporate world has operated under the assumption that parenthood and career advancement are at odds. But as we've explored throughout this chapter, that assumption is not just outdated, it's fundamentally incorrect. Parenthood doesn't diminish leadership potential; it enhances it.

The very challenges that parents navigate daily—crisis management, prioritization, negotiation, emotional intelligence, resilience, and adaptability—are the same competencies that define great leaders. These skills aren't developed in a classroom or a corporate leadership seminar; they are honed in the real-world, high-stakes environment of parenting.

By breaking free from the outdated perception that parenthood is a career setback, businesses can unlock a vast pool of highly skilled, emotionally intelligent, and adaptable leaders. The question is no longer whether working parents can thrive in leadership, it's whether companies are ready to recognize the leadership excellence that is already in front of them.

Key Takeaways

- **Parenthood naturally cultivates critical leadership skills.** Crisis management, prioritization, emotional intelligence, and negotiation—all developed in the parenting crucible—are among the most valued skills companies seek.
- **Companies often overlook working mothers as leadership candidates.** Despite mother and father's enhanced ability to navigate complex, high-pressure situations, it is the mother that is too often assumed to be less committed to career or more distracted by family to step into leadership roles. Meanwhile the father, if they do not take full advantage of leave, is often rewarded.
- **Organizations benefit when they recognize and support the leadership growth that comes with parenthood.** Companies that offer opportunities and support to working parents will gain a competitive advantage in talent retention and team performance.
- **Working parents should confidently articulate the complementary relationship between parenthood and leadership skills.** Outlining the parenting experiences that have strengthened their leadership abilities helps working parents highlight their unique qualifications and find opportunities to apply them in their careers.
- **The modern workplace must shift its perspective on working parents.** Seeing parenthood as a leadership accelerator rather than a career detour allows companies to cultivate top talent and foster stronger, more creative, and more resilient teams.

Reflection

1. How has parenthood (or caregiving) strengthened your leadership abilities in ways you didn't expect?

2. Have you observed a working parent demonstrate exceptional leadership skills in your workplace? What stood out?
3. In what ways could your organization better recognize and support the leadership development that occurs through parenthood?
4. How can managers shift their perception of working parents to see them as high-potential leaders rather than employees with added constraints?
5. What specific skills have you gained through parenting that you can intentionally apply to your career growth?

8 | NAVIGATING LOGISTICS

When we think about parental leave, we often focus on the emotional journey: preparing for a new child, adjusting to a shifting identity, and embracing the joys and challenges of parenthood. But behind every smooth transition into and out of parental leave, there is something far less romantic but equally critical: logistics.

For many employees, the prospect of stepping away from work for weeks or months can feel overwhelming. Who will cover their responsibilities? Will their career take a hit? How will they manage the transition back? On the other side, managers must ensure business continuity, maintain team morale, and support an employee's return in a way that benefits both the individual and the organization. These concerns are not just theoretical; they are the real, everyday challenges that working parents and their employers face.

The key to making parental leave work—for employees, managers, and teams—is early planning, open communication, and flexibility. The more structured the approach, the smoother the transition. A well-prepared leave minimizes disruption, supports career progression, and ensures that returning employees feel confident and valued.

This chapter provides a practical, step-by-step guide for both employees and managers navigating parental leave. We'll break the leave period into three critical phases:

- **Nesting:** The pre-leave period where employees and managers plan for a smooth transition, from handing off workloads to setting clear expectations.

- **The fourth trimester:** The time away from work, where employees adjust to their new role as parents and managers maintain team cohesion while respecting leave boundaries.
- **Returnship:** The reintegration period, where employees come back to work, reclaim their professional identity, and establish a sustainable work–life balance.

Parental leave is not an absence—it is a transition. A well-managed leave can strengthen careers, enhance leadership skills, and even improve workplace culture. By treating parental leave as a strategic, well-supported process, organizations can retain top talent, boost employee loyalty, and foster a more inclusive and productive workplace. According to the National Partnership for Women & Families, companies that implement paid parental leave policies experience a 4.6 percent increase in revenue and a 6.8 percent boost in profit per full-time-equivalent employee—demonstrating that supporting new parents can meaningfully enhance workplace productivity and financial performance.[1]

The partnership between the expectant parent and their manager is a critical factor in a successful parental leave. In our interviews, we have found that true partnership, with clear communication and good planning, is surprisingly rare. This can be due to many factors: fear on the part of the expecting parent, a manager's preconceived notions or lack of clarity about policy, or simply insufficient systemic guidance on how to implement what might be a very well-thought-out and extensive leave policy. The absence of a strong partnership between parent-to-be and manager is a lost opportunity that can be easily remedied with a deeper understanding of the stages of a parental leave transition and specific tools and strategies. Whether you are an expecting parent or a manager preparing to support a team member through this transition, this chapter provides practical tools, real-world strategies, and actionable insights to make parental leave work—for everyone.

Nesting: Preparing for Parental Leave

The months leading up to parental leave are a time of preparation—not just at home, but at work. This phase, which we call nesting, is about laying the groundwork for a smooth transition, ensuring that both employees and managers feel confident in the plan for leave and return.

For expecting parents, nesting involves communicating with their employer, planning a structured handoff, and setting expectations for their leave and eventual return. For managers, this phase is about supporting the employee's transition while maintaining workflow and team stability. A well-managed nesting phase ensures that parental leave is not disruptive but instead a well-integrated part of the employee's career journey.

A thoughtful approach to this phase makes all the difference. Without clear communication and proactive planning, uncertainty can create unnecessary stress for both the individual and the organization. But with the right preparation, leave becomes a manageable transition, one that strengthens both the employee's career and the company's ability to support working parents.

Preparing for Leave as an Employee

One of the first and most significant decisions an expecting parent makes in the workplace is when to share the news. The timing of this announcement is influenced by several factors, including company culture, the nature of one's role, and personal comfort levels. Some employees wait until after the first trimester, while others disclose earlier due to medical needs or workplace accommodations. Regardless of timing, approaching this conversation with confidence and a clear plan helps ensure a positive response.

When speaking with a manager, it's beneficial to frame parental leave as a well-structured transition rather than a disruption. This means reassuring leadership of your continued commitment to your role and providing some initial thinking, such as a possible road map for how work will be managed in your absence. For employees in leadership or highly specialized roles, early discussions allow more time to develop a thoughtful coverage plan.

As an expectant parent, you will want this conversation to demonstrate that you intend to work in partnership with your manager and your team to ensure the best possible transition.

Once the announcement is made, handoff planning becomes a critical next step. This planning will likely be done in partnership with your manager, as they need to be fully on board with changes in the workflow and the way the entire team will be impacted. A well-executed transition ensures that projects and responsibilities continue seamlessly, while the disruption for colleagues is minimized. Identifying key tasks, documenting processes, and training temporary replacements help create a sense of continuity. Employees should consider hosting a dedicated handoff meeting before their departure to ensure clarity and alignment.

In addition to planning for the way work will be managed, employee and manager must set expectations about communication during leave. Some employees prefer complete disconnection, while others appreciate occasional updates. Being upfront about communication preferences prevents misunderstandings and ensures that both the employee and employer are aligned on boundaries during this period.

Another often overlooked but essential part of the nesting phase is discussing return-to-work plans before leave begins. Even if these plans evolve, setting an initial framework signals to the organization that the employee intends to return and helps managers think ahead about reintegration. Conversations about career progression, potential flexible schedules, or phased returns can help ensure a smooth transition back to the workplace.

Supporting Parental Leave as a Manager

For managers, an employee's parental leave should never feel like an unexpected challenge. When organizations foster a culture where leave is normalized and well planned, the transition becomes seamless for both the individual and the broader team.

Managers play a key role in creating an environment where employees feel comfortable discussing and preparing for leave without fear of career repercussions. Just as the expecting parent should approach their manager as a partner in this process, the manager should engage the expecting parent in a way that demonstrates that they are working together to create the best possible experience for everyone, including the entire team.

The first step in supporting an employee through this transition is setting a positive tone. Employees should feel assured that taking leave is not only accepted but encouraged. Reinforcing that parental leave does not equate to career stagnation or diminished opportunities helps alleviate any concerns employees may have about stepping away.

Once an employee announces their leave, a manager's focus should shift to facilitating a structured transition. This involves working collaboratively with the employee to determine how their responsibilities will be managed during their absence. Some work may be redistributed among colleagues, while other tasks may require a temporary replacement. A manager must engage this planning process thoughtfully, as it will impact team dynamics in a broader context than any individual parental leave. Ensuring that no single team member is overburdened by additional responsibilities prevents burnout and maintains overall team morale.

A successful transition also requires clear documentation and proactive planning. Encouraging the employee to create reference materials, project timelines, or a transition guide ensures that those who step in can confidently manage the workload. Scheduling a final handoff meeting before leave begins provides an opportunity to align on any outstanding details.

Equally important is planning for the employee's return before they leave. This is not like a vacation leave when someone refreshed jumps right back in at the end of their leave. Too often, organizations focus exclusively on preparing for an employee's departure without considering how to reintegrate them effectively. Discussing career path expectations before leave begins signals to the employee that they remain valued and that their role will continue to evolve upon their return. Ensuring that performance evaluations, promotions, or leadership opportunities are not sidelined because of leave helps reinforce the message that parenthood and professional growth can coexist.

By establishing a clear return-to-work plan—even if it remains flexible—managers can remove much of the uncertainty that employees may feel about coming back. Simple actions, such as setting a check-in conversation a few weeks before their return or keeping the employee lightly informed about workplace developments, help bridge the transition.

Laying the Foundation for a Smooth Transition

The nesting phase is a crucial period that sets the tone for how both the employee and the organization experience parental leave. For employees, early communication, a well-planned hand-off, and clear leave expectations provide structure and peace of mind. Managers who foster a culture of support, create a structured transition plan, and proactively consider reentry ensure that the leave period is a seamless part of an employee's career journey rather than a career interruption.

When nesting is approached with strategic planning and collaboration, parental leave becomes an asset rather than a challenge—one that strengthens both individuals and organizations.

The Fourth Trimester: Navigating Life During Leave

Parental leave is often thought of as time away from work, but it is far more than an absence. It is a transition, one that is as critical to an employee's long-term success as any other major career shift. This twelve-week period after birth, often called the fourth trimester, is a time of profound adjustment, both personally and professionally. It is a phase marked by new routines, shifting priorities, and, for many, an evolving relationship with work.

How employees and managers handle this transition determines not only the success of the leave itself but also the ease of reintegration. Employees must establish boundaries while staying informed in ways that serve their needs. Managers must respect leave while ensuring that employees feel connected to the organization when they are ready to return. The goal is not just to navigate time away, but to lay the groundwork for a smooth return.

Too much attention is paid to the number of weeks of leave a parent plans to take; though that is certainly important, it is not the only factor in a culture that successfully supports working parent. Leave that covers the entire fourth trimester is a game changer. There is a lot of research on the long-term impact on children when leave is less than twelve weeks for the primary caregiver. For example, research by the Brant County Health Unit in Ontario found that mothers returning to work full time before twelve weeks was associated with an increase in problem behaviors and poorer language development by the time they reach kindergarten.[2] The amount of available paid leave is only part of the picture, however; also critical are the other supports wrapped around leave that will create a more welcoming culture.

Adjusting to Leave as an Employee

The early weeks of parental leave are a paradox. On one hand, everything is new—schedules, priorities, even identity. On the other, time moves at an unfamiliar pace, with days blending into nights. Many employees enter leave intending to fully detach from work, only to find themselves wondering what they are missing. Others expect to stay lightly engaged but quickly realize that even the smallest work tasks can feel overwhelming in the fog of sleep deprivation.

The most important thing employees can do in the early weeks of leave is set and honor their boundaries. While some may choose complete disconnection, others might prefer occasional updates. Regardless of approach, defining expectations in advance prevents work from creeping in unexpectedly. If an employee has agreed to be contacted for critical issues, it is essential to clarify what constitutes "critical" to avoid unnecessary disruptions.

Equally important is managing the emotional impact of stepping away from work. For high achievers, the sudden shift from professional productivity to the unpredictability of newborn care can be jarring. It is common to feel a sense of professional detachment or even insecurity about one's place in the organization. Employees who have spent years defining themselves by their contributions at work may struggle with the temporary loss of that identity. A helpful mindset shift is to recognize that this time is not about career stagnation but about building resilience, adaptability, and leadership in a new form—skills that will serve them long after they return.

As leave progresses, some employees may find value in staying lightly informed about workplace developments. Whether that means reading company updates, checking in with a trusted colleague, or participating in designated "keep-in-touch" days, these small actions can help ease the transition back. However, these updates should always be on the employee's terms. There is no professional advantage to feeling tethered to work during a period meant for recovery, bonding, and adjustment.

For employees who start to think about their return midway through leave, reflecting on what they want that return to look like can be helpful. Some may feel ready to reengage fully, while others may realize they need a phased approach. Having this clarity before the return conversation with their manager allows for a more confident and intentional reintegration.

Respecting Leave as a Manager

While employees focus on adjusting to parenthood, managers must navigate the delicate balance of maintaining business continuity while respecting the integrity of an employee's leave. Too little communication can leave employees feeling disconnected from their professional identity, while too much can erode the benefits of leave entirely. The best managers approach this period with intentionality, respect, and a long-term perspective.

The most fundamental rule is simple: leave is leave. Employees should not be contacted unless it is for a pre-agreed reason, and certainly never for routine matters that could wait. This requires discipline, particularly in organizations where employees on leave have historically been expected to remain accessible. Setting clear expectations with the team about what constitutes an appropriate reason to reach out prevents unnecessary disruptions.

At the same time, managers should ensure that employees on leave do not feel like they are returning to a completely unfamiliar environment. One way to do this is by offering a structured but optional check-in before their return. This could be a brief conversation to update them on any major team changes, company shifts, or projects they may be stepping back into. However, this should always be positioned as an invitation rather than an obligation. The purpose is to create a sense of inclusion, not pressure.

Another critical responsibility for managers during this time is proactively managing team dynamics in the employee's absence. Parental leave should not become a point of resentment among colleagues who are temporarily carrying an additional workload. Setting clear expectations about the temporary nature of these adjustments helps prevent frustration. Equally important is reinforcing to the entire team that leave is not a professional detour but an integral part of an employee's long-term career at the organization.

Finally, managers should begin thinking about reintegration well before the employee's return. This means ensuring that the employee's role remains intact, their career trajectory is not quietly deprioritized, and their reentry is as smooth as possible. Managers must take care not to make assumptions about what a returning employee might want or need, or what their near-future goals are. Those managers who take a long-term approach to parental leave understand that the way an employee experiences this transition directly impacts their engagement, loyalty, and future contributions to the company.

Returnship: Successfully Reintegrating into Work

Returning to work after parental leave is often described as a second major transition, and it can be as complex and emotionally charged as the leave itself. This period, which we call returnship, is not just about resuming work; it's about rebuilding confidence, reestablishing professional identity, and redefining work–life balance in a sustainable way.

For employees, this means navigating the logistical, emotional, and career-related challenges that come with reentry. For managers, it involves ensuring that returning employees feel valued, supported, and positioned for long-term success rather than treated as if they are starting over. The companies that get this right retain top talent, foster deeper employee loyalty, and create an environment where both work and parenthood are valued.

Reestablishing Work Rhythms as an Employee

The first days and weeks back at work are a delicate balancing act. Employees often return eager to reengage but may also face new logistical hurdles, shifts in priorities, and lingering fatigue from the demands of early parenthood. Even for those who feel excited to be back, the shift from full-time caregiving to professional responsibilities can be disorienting.

A successful returnship begins with realistic expectations. Many employees assume they will immediately operate at their pre-leave capacity, only to find that work feels unfamiliar or that their energy levels fluctuate in ways they did not anticipate. Recognizing that there is a natural adjustment period helps prevent frustration and burnout.

One of the most effective strategies for a smooth transition is easing back in gradually, when possible. Some employees benefit from a phased return, such as starting with reduced hours or remote flexibility in the first few weeks. Others may prefer to return full-time but with a transition plan that prioritizes reintegration rather than immediate high-stakes projects.

Communication is also key. Setting clear expectations with a manager about workload, availability, and any needed flexibility ensures that potential concerns are addressed before they become problems. For employees who need accommodations—whether for childcare schedules, lactation breaks, or ongoing sleep challenges—being proactive about discussing these needs helps create mutual understanding and practical solutions.

Beyond logistics, one of the biggest challenges employees face in returnship is reclaiming professional identity. After months away, it's common to experience a sense of distance from one's work persona. Some employees worry that their contributions have been diminished or that their long-term ambitions have been called into question. To combat this, it can be helpful to identify early opportunities for visibility and impact, whether that's taking ownership of a project, reengaging with key stakeholders, or contributing fresh insights from time away.

Reintegration is not just about proving capability; it's about redefining how work fits into life post-parenthood. Employees who take a strategic approach to returnship—by setting boundaries, maintaining flexibility, and advocating for their ongoing growth—are more likely to find long-term success in both their professional and personal lives.

Creating a Supportive Reentry as a Manager

For managers, returnship is an opportunity to reinforce that parental leave is not a career setback but a natural part of an employee's professional trajectory. The way an employee is welcomed back directly impacts their engagement, retention, and long-term contributions to the company.

The first and most critical step in this process is ensuring that the returning employee does not feel like they are starting over. Too often, employees come back to find that their projects have been reassigned, their responsibilities have been shifted, or they are no longer included in key conversations. Some may even return to find they no longer have the same office space or the same team. Even when changes made during leave have been necessary, it is essential to communicate a clear plan for reintegration.

A well-managed return begins before the employee's first day back. Scheduling a reentry conversation in the weeks leading up to their return provides an opportunity to discuss workload, expectations, and any changes that have taken place. This check-in should be framed as an open dialogue, allowing the employee to share their preferences for how they would like to reintegrate.

During the employee's first days back, managers should focus on reaffirming their value. Simple but meaningful gestures such as a welcome-back message, a team lunch, or a one-on-one meeting to reconnect help ease the transition. More importantly, managers should ensure that the employee is stepping back into meaningful work rather than being sidelined with minor tasks under the assumption that they need time to "catch up."

Beyond the initial return, career-path discussions should be a priority. One of the most damaging but common workplace biases is the assumption that new parents are less ambitious or less willing to take on leadership roles. Managers should actively counteract this assumption by continuing to involve returning employees in high-impact projects, professional development opportunities, and strategic conversations. If a manager assumes that an employee's career trajectory has changed, they are making a decision on the employee's behalf rather than letting them define their own path.

At the same time, managers should acknowledge that the needs of returning employees may have evolved. Offering flexibility, when possible, reinforces that the company supports performance over presenteeism. If an employee's schedule needs adjusting—whether for daycare drop-offs, remote workdays, or altered meeting times—approaching these conversations with a problem-solving mindset rather than a rigid framework ensures that both the employee and the business continue to thrive.

Finally, managers should be aware of hidden biases that can emerge post-leave. Unintentional micro-messages—such as assuming a new parent does not want travel opportunities or excluding them from late-day meetings—can send signals that their career is no longer a priority. A conscious effort to treat parental leave as a normal, expected part of the career journey helps reinforce an inclusive workplace culture.

Sustaining Career Growth After Leave

The true test of returnship is not in the first few weeks back but in how an employee's career continues to evolve in the months that follow. Employees who return with a clear vision of how they want to reengage, a willingness to communicate their needs, and a focus on long-term success set themselves up for stability and growth. Those who are able to redefine work–life integration in a way that aligns with their values and goals will sustain both performance and well-being.

For managers, a successful returnship leaves no question about an employee's value, capability, and future at the organization. The companies that thrive in today's evolving workplace are those that recognize parenthood as an asset rather than a liability—one that enhances leadership skills, strengthens decision making, and deepens resilience.

When returnship is handled with thoughtfulness, strategy, and a long-term mindset, parental leave ceases to be a career disruption. Instead, it becomes a chapter of professional growth—one that strengthens both individuals and the organizations they serve.

Conclusion: Making Parental Leave Work for Everyone

Parental leave is not just time away from work—it is a structured transition that, when managed well, benefits both employees and organizations. The process of preparing for leave, stepping away, and returning to work is an opportunity to strengthen leadership, enhance organizational culture, and reinforce a workplace that values both professional excellence and personal well-being.

Too often, parental leave is framed as an interruption or a challenge to be managed. In reality, it is a natural and expected part of an employee's career journey. When companies approach leave with intention, planning, and a long-term perspective, they retain top talent, reinforce employee loyalty, and build a stronger, more inclusive workforce. Aetna's expansion of maternity leave led to a rise in the percentage of women returning to work—from 77 percent to 91 percent—highlighting how more generous parental leave policies can significantly boost female workforce participation.

For employees, a well-planned leave sets the stage for a confident and seamless return. Those who approach the nesting phase with clear communication, strategic handoffs, and proactive career planning create a smoother transition both into and out of leave. During the fourth trimester, establishing boundaries and embracing the shift in identity ensures that leave remains a time of growth, not disconnection. And in returnship, taking an active role in reintegration—by setting expectations, seeking meaningful contributions, and aligning work with evolving priorities—ensures long-term success.

For managers, the role is just as critical. Leaders who support employees through these transitions create teams that are more engaged, resilient, and high-performing. A company's approach to parental leave is a reflection of its culture. Those that treat leave as an accepted, career-sustaining event—not a professional setback—are the ones that retain and grow their best talent.

Organizations that normalize parental leave, set clear policies, and offer structured support will find that they are creating a better experience not only for parents but for their entire workforce. By recognizing that the skills employees gain through parenthood—resilience, adaptability, prioritization—are directly transferable to their professional roles, businesses can leverage, rather than lose, the full potential of working parents.

Parental leave should never be a point of uncertainty, frustration, or career derailment. Instead, it should be seen as an investment in people, in leadership development, and in the future of work itself. Companies that understand this will not only create a better workplace for parents but will drive stronger business outcomes, attract top talent, and build a culture that employees are proud to be part of.

Parental leave isn't a challenge to be managed. It's an opportunity to be embraced, so let's look at a practical guide that helps to summarize this chapter

Three Months Before Leave: Laying the Groundwork
This is the time to shift from announcement to planning mode.
- Meet with your manager and, if possible, HR to begin discussing your expected leave dates.
- Start drafting a transition plan: What work will need to be handed off? Who might take the lead on key responsibilities? Where are your systems or processes documented?
- Clarify how and when you'd like to communicate during leave (if at all).
- Schedule key pre-leave deadlines (e.g., last client handoff, final report, team meetings) well in advance to prevent a rush at the end.
- Begin mapping out your ideal return-to-work rhythm. Would a phased return or flexible schedule be helpful?

One Month Before Leave: Finalizing the Plan
This is your window to lock in the handoff.
- Share your transition plan in writing, including a summary of active projects, important deadlines, and any work-in-progress documentation.
- Confirm out-of-office contacts for your stakeholders, and prepare email auto-replies.
- Hold handoff meetings with teammates or direct reports who will be stepping in.
- Have a final alignment meeting with your manager to walk through expectations, coverage, and communication preferences.

- Let your team know how to best support you during this time and what to expect in your absence. Transparency helps reduce second-guessing or overcompensation.

During Leave: Protecting the Pause

This is not a time to check in—unless you've expressly chosen to.

- If you've agreed to periodic updates, clarify who will reach out and when. This might be limited to a single check-in around your intended return date.
- Trust the systems and people you've prepared. Letting go is part of the handoff.
- HR should be available in case any changes to your leave or return timeline arise (e.g., health considerations, extended bonding time).

Three Weeks Before Return: Re-Onboarding

This is the time to shift your mindset gently back toward work.

- Reach out to your manager to schedule a pre-return check-in.
- Request a brief summary of what's changed in your absence: team structure, key initiatives, leadership updates, open projects.
- Clarify your first week's schedule and whether any accommodations are needed (e.g., lactation space, remote days, childcare start date).
- Revisit your goals: what would a successful first month back look like?

First 30 Days Back: Returnship, Not Whiplash

Reentry is not just about catching up—it's about reconnecting.

- Don't overbook your first week. Allow time for recalibration.
- Schedule 1:1s with colleagues, clients, and stakeholders to reconnect personally and professionally.

- Check in with your manager at the end of the first week, and again after 30 days, to revisit goals and adjust support if needed.
- Reflect on what's changed for you—and what hasn't. This is often a period of reevaluation and realignment, not just reentry.

For sample templates to help you navigate the logistics of leave, please visit www.TheParenthoodAdvantage.com.

Key Takeaways

- **Parental leave is a transition, not an absence.** A well-planned leave benefits both employees and organizations by ensuring continuity and long-term career growth.
- **Communication and planning are essential.** Employees should proactively structure their handoffs, set expectations, and discuss their return plans before they leave.
- **Managers play a critical role in making leave successful.** Supportive leadership, structured transitions, and reintegration strategies help retain talent and build an inclusive workplace.
- **The fourth trimester is a time of adjustment.** Employees should establish boundaries while balancing personal recovery and professional reentry at their own pace.
- **Returnship should be intentional.** Employees and managers must collaborate to ensure a smooth transition back, avoiding career stagnation and reinforcing long-term opportunities.

Reflection

1. **For employees:** What steps can you take to ensure a smooth transition before, during, and after parental leave?
2. **For managers:** How can you proactively support an employee's parental leave while maintaining team productivity and morale?
3. What biases—explicit or unconscious—exist in your workplace regarding parental leave, and how can they be addressed?
4. What strategies can organizations implement to ensure that returning parents are reintegrated effectively and not sidelined in their careers?
5. How does your workplace culture influence employees' decisions to take full parental leave, and what changes could make leave more accessible and accepted?

9 | THE CORPORATE ROLE

A decade from now, when we look back at how workplaces evolved, we may ask ourselves: Did organizations seize the opportunity to broaden the definition of inclusion and embrace the full potential of working parents, or did they cling to outdated notions of the goals of parents, and how becoming a parent affects productivity and career development?

The workplace has always reflected societal values, yet it also plays a critical role in shaping them. In the past, companies operated as if parenthood and professional ambition were incompatible, especially for women. But today, as workforce demographics shift, labor shortages loom, and new generations demand more flexibility, the business world faces a choice: evolve to support working parents or risk losing the very talent that fuels innovation and growth.

The companies that will thrive are the ones that don't see parenthood as a zero-sum game, but instead recognize the parenthood advantage—the leadership skills, resilience, and efficiency that come with raising children—and create environments that not only accommodate but actively leverage these strengths.

The Business as Culture Maker

Culture is not just an abstract concept; it's a set of behaviors, mindsets, and expectations reinforced through policies, leadership, and everyday workplace interactions. While government policies provide the legal framework for parental rights, it's businesses that ultimately determine whether parents succeed or struggle in the workplace. A parental leave policy may exist on paper, but if a culture of silent judgment penalizes employees for taking it, the policy is meaningless.

Consider the story of Esteban, a project manager who took paternity leave only to be pulled into a challenging client situation while he was still out. Despite clear policies in place, the expectation that he remain "on call" signaled that caregiving was secondary to his work responsibilities. This is a common experience, one that reveals a gap between stated policies and actual workplace culture. On the flip side, companies that embed true support for parents create environments where employees feel secure in prioritizing family when needed, knowing it won't derail their careers.

Companies play a profound role in shaping not just employee experiences but societal norms. When organizations openly celebrate fathers taking leave, they accelerate the normalization of caregiving as a shared responsibility. When they promote mothers into leadership roles while supporting their work–life integration, they dismantle the myth that parenthood diminishes ambition.

This chapter explores how companies can lead the shift toward parent-supportive workplaces, not just through policies but through systemic changes that shape culture. We'll examine why businesses must take the lead in making parenthood a workplace advantage rather than a liability. We'll describe how organizations can embed support for parents into their structures, policies, and leadership models, and look at the next evolution of work—what the future holds for working parents and the companies that support them. Finally, we include a call to action: now is the time for companies and leaders to ensure they don't fall behind.

Such action is not just about being a "family-friendly" company—it's about ensuring long-term business success in a rapidly changing world. Organizations that adapt will gain a competitive edge in talent attraction, retention, and innovation. Those that resist will struggle to keep up in an era where the boundaries between work and life are being redefined.

As we conclude this book, the message is clear: companies have a unique and urgent role to play in building workplaces that recognize, support, and maximize the strengths of working parents. The question now is, will they rise to the challenge?

The Corporate Imperative:
Why Organizations Must Lead the Change

Supporting working parents is not just a moral imperative—it's a business necessity. In earlier chapters, we've described the research data that creates a strong business case. The bottom line is that the modern workforce is changing, and organizations that fail to adapt risk falling behind in the competition for top talent, innovation, and long-term sustainability.

The Economic and Demographic Reality

For years, businesses operated under the assumption that work and family should remain separate spheres. That mindset is no longer viable. In countries around the world, birth rates are declining, populations are aging, and talent shortages are becoming more pronounced. Employers can no longer afford to ignore the needs of working parents if they want to attract and retain skilled professionals.

A striking example comes from Japan and South Korea, where corporate cultures historically discouraged parental leave, especially for fathers. Birth rates have plummeted to record lows, threatening long-term economic stability. Governments have since scrambled to create incentives for work–family balance, but cultural change within corporations has been slow. By contrast, Nordic countries, where paid parental leave and workplace flexibility are the norm, have maintained higher birth rates and economic participation from both mothers and fathers. The lesson is clear: when businesses fail to support parents, economies suffer.

The United States is facing its own reckoning. In a labor market where over 80 percent of employees will become parents at some point in their careers, companies that continue to see parenthood as a disruption rather than a long-term asset will struggle to retain key talent.

The Competitive Advantage of Parent-Supportive Workplaces
Organizations that actively create parent-supportive environments enjoy significant benefits:

- **Higher retention and lower turnover costs:** Losing an employee costs, on average, one-half to two times their annual salary in hiring and training expenses. Companies with strong parental support programs see higher retention rates among new parents, which reduces costs and maintains institutional knowledge.
- **Stronger leadership pipelines:** Parenthood develops critical workplace skills—resilience, multitasking, crisis management, and empathy—all of which translate into stronger leadership. Companies that recognize and nurture these skills build deeper leadership pipelines and improve succession planning.
- **Higher engagement and productivity:** Employees who feel supported in their personal lives bring more focus and energy to their work. In contrast, workplaces that pressure parents to "leave their family responsibilities at the door" create burnout, disengagement, and ultimately lower performance.

Companies that support working parents aren't just fostering goodwill, they're investing in long-term business success.

The Risk of Stagnation: What Happens to Companies That Don't Adapt?
While forward-thinking organizations are leveraging parenthood as an advantage, others remain stuck in outdated models of work. These companies are facing growing risks:

- **Losing talent to more progressive competitors:**
  Employees today—especially millennials and Gen Zers—
  actively seek out workplaces that respect work–life
  integration. Companies that ignore this shift will see top
  talent walk away.
- **Public and employee backlash:** The rise of platforms
  like Glassdoor and LinkedIn means corporate culture is
  more transparent than ever. Companies that fail to support
  parents risk reputational damage and difficulty in hiring.
- **Lower innovation and weaker leadership pipelines:**
  Organizations that undervalue the problem-solving skills,
  adaptability, and emotional intelligence of parents are
  failing to cultivate some of their most effective leaders.

The Role of Leadership: Why Change Must Come from the Top

Policy changes alone won't shift workplace culture. The most
successful transformations happen when executive leadership
actively champions a parent-supportive environment.

Consider Colin, the CEO of a midsize tech company, who
took a full three months of paternity leave when his first child was
born. By doing so, he set a powerful precedent, demonstrating
that caregiving was not just acceptable but valued. His decision
had ripple effects throughout the company: the following year,
paternity leave uptake among male employees increased by 40
percent, and retention among new parents improved significantly.

Leaders don't just set policies—they set norms. When managers openly discuss their experiences as parents, when they
respect caregiving responsibilities, and when they advocate for
workplace flexibility, they create a culture where employees feel
supported, rather than penalized, for balancing work and family.

A truly parent-supportive workplace is not built through
isolated policies or surface-level benefits. It requires a systemic
shift, a transformation in culture, leadership, and organizational
design that ensures working parents can thrive. Companies
that succeed in this effort recognize that supporting parents is

not about temporary accommodations but rather about struc-turing the workplace in a way that maximizes the strengths, engagement, and long-term retention of employees who are also caregivers.

The business world stands at a crossroads. The companies that recognize parenthood as an asset—not an inconvenience—will be the ones that thrive in the future economy. The question is not whether workplaces can support working parents, but whether they will.

Shifting Workplace Culture

A company's parental leave policy may look generous on paper, but if employees feel they will be penalized for taking it, the policy is meaningless. Culture is defined not just by what is written in a handbook but by the unspoken norms, leadership behaviors, and workplace expectations that signal what is truly valued. The shift to a parent-supportive culture must be intentional, and it must come from the top.

One of the most effective ways to drive cultural change is through visible leadership. When senior executives take parental leave, openly discuss their experiences as working parents, and advocate for flexibility, they send a clear message: caregiving is not a liability. It is an integral part of life, and it does not diminish an employee's career potential. At a consumer products firm, retention among new parents had been lagging, despite strong benefits on paper. Women, in particular, were leaving at higher rates, citing an unspoken expectation that taking advantage of flexible work options would be viewed as a sign of reduced com-mitment. The company responded by launching an executive sponsorship program in which senior leaders actively encouraged employees to take the leave and flexibility they needed. The result was a 35 percent increase in retention among new parents and a 20 percent rise in female leadership representation.

Beyond leadership, organizations can normalize parenthood in professional spaces by making working parents more visible.

Internal newsletters can highlight employees who are successfully balancing work and family. Parental status can be acknowledged in bios, signaling that caregiving is a valued part of an employee's identity rather than something to be hidden. Even the way flexibility is framed matters—when companies position flexibility not as an accommodation but as a strategic advantage that fosters productivity and innovation, it changes the narrative from one of exception-making to one of business intelligence.

Redesigning Parental Policies to Reflect Real Needs

While culture sets the tone, policies provide the foundation for a parent-supportive workplace. The most effective policies recognize that parenthood is diverse and that families come in many forms, whether through birth, adoption, surrogacy, or caregiving responsibilities that extend beyond infancy.

Companies at the forefront of this shift are moving away from traditional maternity leave structures and offering gender-neutral, fully paid parental leave for all caregivers. This approach not only reduces stigma around caregiving but also helps businesses retain talent by ensuring all employees, regardless of gender or family structure, have equal opportunities to care for their children without penalty.

Phased return-to-work options are another policy that can make an enormous difference. The abrupt shift from full-time parental leave to full-time work can be overwhelming, often leading to burnout or attrition. Companies that allow employees to return gradually—perhaps starting with reduced hours or remote work—ease the transition and improve retention. Similarly, policies that support parents beyond the early months, such as backup childcare options and flexible scheduling for school-age children, reflect the reality that caregiving needs evolve.

When policies are designed with these realities in mind, they become powerful talent magnets. Spotify, for example, introduced a six-month, fully paid parental leave policy, with the option to take leave flexibly over three years. The policy not only improved retention but also positioned the company as an employer of choice, attracting top-tier talent who prioritized work–life balance.

Equipping Managers to Support Working Parents

Even the most progressive policies will fail if managers are not equipped to implement them effectively. Many leaders want to support their team members but lack the training, tools, and confidence to do so.

Bias against parents in performance evaluations remains one of the greatest barriers to career advancement for working parents. Employees who become parents, particularly women, are often subtly (or not so subtly) perceived as less ambitious, less available, or more distracted, despite research showing that parenthood actually enhances leadership skills.

Training managers to recognize and eliminate these biases is essential. One financial services firm introduced mandatory parental support training for managers, teaching them how to offer flexibility equitably, hold open conversations about career goals with new parents, and proactively support employees returning from leave. The results were striking: employee satisfaction among working parents increased by 25 percent, and promotions among women returning from leave rose by 40 percent.

Beyond training, companies should encourage "stay conversations" with employees before and after they take leave. Rather than assuming an employee will downshift or step back after becoming a parent, managers should ask about their career aspirations, offer support, and ensure they feel valued. These conversations help retain talent and reinforce the message that parenthood does not mean the end of career growth.

Rethinking Performance Metrics

For too long, workplace success has been measured by availability rather than actual performance. Employees who are constantly online, stay late, and appear always "on" are often perceived as more dedicated, even if their work output does not reflect it. This outdated metric disproportionately penalizes parents, who may have time constraints but who also bring to their roles unparalleled efficiency, problem-solving skills, and adaptability.

Companies that truly support working parents must shift from measuring hours to measuring outcomes. When performance is evaluated based on results, deliverables, and strategic contributions rather than the number of hours logged at a desk, a more equitable and inclusive work environment emerges.

One leading software company made this shift by adopting a Results-Only Work Environment (ROWE), where employees were judged entirely on outcomes rather than rigid schedules. The impact was profound: productivity increased by 30 percent, voluntary turnover dropped by 50 percent, and employee engagement—especially among working parents—rose significantly.

To reinforce this mindset shift, companies should recognize parent employees as leaders and contributors. Celebrating their achievements in internal communications, incorporating parental leadership skills into promotion criteria, and actively engaging working parents all help reframe parenthood as an asset rather than a liability.

A Systemic Approach for Long-Term Impact

What separates companies that truly support working parents from those that simply check a box is the depth of their commitment. A single progressive policy will not create lasting change unless it is woven into a broader system that includes cultural reinforcement, leadership modeling, and reimagined performance metrics.

The companies that lead in this space understand that investing in working parents is an investment in long-term business success. They don't just accommodate parenthood, they leverage it. They recognize that employees who are parents bring resilience, efficiency, emotional intelligence, and crisis management skills to the table—qualities that drive innovation and leadership.

In the next section, we'll explore what the future holds for workplaces that embrace parenthood as an advantage. As work continues to evolve in the face of technological, demographic, and cultural shifts, companies have an opportunity to redesign the workplace of the future and create one where parenthood is not just accepted, but valued as a strategic strength.

The Next Evolution: Rethinking Work and Family Integration

The workplace has undergone significant transformation in the last few decades, with changes accelerating in the last several years due to the Covid pandemic. But the shifts we've seen so far—remote work, flexible schedules, expanded parental benefits—are only the beginning. As technology, demographics, and cultural expectations continue to evolve, companies will need to rethink not just how they accommodate working parents, but how they actively integrate parenthood into the very structure of work itself.

Forward-thinking organizations are already recognizing that the future of work will be more fluid, human centric, and results driven than ever before. The companies that adapt will be the ones that attract and retain top talent in an increasingly competitive labor market. The ones that don't will struggle to acquire and retain the talent necessary to survive.

Beyond Work–life Balance: A Seamless Integration

For years, the conversation around working parents has been framed as a work–life balance issue, a perpetual juggling act between two competing priorities. But the most successful workplaces of the future will not see work and parenthood as forces in opposition; they will see them as mutually reinforcing.

Already, companies that are on the cutting edge of workplace design are experimenting with models that blend work and caregiving in new ways. Instead of expecting employees to fit their family lives around rigid work structures, they are redesigning work to fit around the realities of modern families.

For example, some organizations are beginning to offer "work-near-home" models, where employees can work from coworking spaces with on-site childcare, eliminating the need for long commutes and making caregiving transitions seamless. Others are rethinking traditional work schedules altogether, shifting away from rigid nine-to-five expectations toward task- and outcome-based work, allowing employees to work when they are most effective.

Some industries are even embracing family-first corporate retreats and team-building events, acknowledging that employees do not leave their identities as parents behind when they enter the workplace. Why should corporate culture pretend otherwise? Instead of expecting parents to miss critical family moments in the name of career advancement, companies are beginning to design professional growth opportunities that acknowledge and include their roles as caregivers.

How AI and Technology Will Reshape Work for Parents

The rise of artificial intelligence (AI) and automation is already reshaping work across industries, but it may have an especially profound impact on working parents. AI-driven tools have the potential to reduce the need for constant availability, allowing employees to accomplish more in less time.

Companies that harness AI effectively will create environments where employees—especially parents—can focus on high-value, strategic work while automating repetitive tasks. This shift will allow for greater flexibility, making it easier than ever for parents to integrate work into their lives in ways that align with their personal and family responsibilities.

Imagine a workplace where AI-assisted scheduling allows employees to set their preferred work hours around school drop-offs and pickups, automatically optimizing meetings and deadlines to fit within those windows. Or a system where AI-generated insights help managers proactively identify employees at risk of burnout, allowing companies to offer targeted support before retention becomes an issue.

The most forward-thinking companies are not asking, "How can parents fit into the workplace?" They are asking, "How can we design work in a way that best utilizes the strengths of parents while maximizing their efficiency and engagement?"

The Rising Demand for Family-First Workplaces

Demographic shifts will also force organizations to rethink their approach to work and caregiving. In many developed countries, birth rates are declining while life expectancy is increasing, leading to a talent shortage and a greater percentage of employees balancing both childcare and eldercare responsibilities. The companies that recognize this shift early and build cultures friendly to caregiving will be the ones that thrive in the coming decades.

At the same time, the newest generations of employees—millennials and Gen Z—are demanding workplaces that reflect their values. These generations are far less willing than their predecessors to accept a work environment that requires them to sacrifice their family lives for career success. They are choosing to work for companies that offer meaningful flexibility, robust parental benefits, and leadership cultures that embrace work–life integration.

Companies that resist these changes risk losing the next generation of top talent. The organizations that succeed will be the ones that actively compete to be the best workplaces for parents, much in the way they have historically competed to offer the highest salaries, the best perks, or the most prestigious brand recognition.

The Ideal Parent-Supportive Workplace of 2035

If we imagine the most progressive, family-first workplace of the future, what might it look like?

• Parental leave will no longer be a "perk"—it will be an expectation, fully paid and available to all caregivers, with equal opportunities for career advancement.

• Work schedules will be driven by outcomes rather than time at a desk. Employees will work in asynchronous, results-oriented ways, allowing parents to maximize efficiency without sacrificing caregiving responsibilities.

• Caregiving support will extend beyond infancy. School-age parenting, eldercare, and multigenerational family responsibilities will be built into workplace policies.

• AI-driven personalization will allow employees to design their work schedules based on their unique family needs.

• Companies will compete to be ranked among the most parent-friendly workplaces, understanding that a reputation for supporting families is a key driver of talent attraction and retention.

This vision is not science fiction—it is already beginning to take shape in some of the world's most innovative companies. Those that embrace this shift now will have a decisive advantage in attracting, retaining, and benefiting from the talents of working parents.

The Future Is Already Here—
Will Companies Lead or Fall Behind?

The companies that embrace the evolving landscape of work and parenthood will be the ones that thrive in the future economy. Those that resist, clinging to outdated structures that fail to recognize the realities of modern employees, will find themselves unable to compete.

The question is no longer whether workplaces will change—it is how quickly and effectively companies will adapt. Organizations that take the lead in designing work around the needs of working parents will be the ones that reap the benefits of a more engaged, loyal, and high-performing workforce.

As we approach the conclusion of this book, we return to the central question: Will companies view parenthood as a burden to be managed or an asset to be leveraged? The answer will define not just the future of work but the very foundation of business success in the decades to come. One thing is clear: the way companies approach parenthood will define their success in the future of work. The question is no longer whether organizations can support working parents, but whether they will.

A Call to Action

Workplace transformation does not happen in a vacuum. It begins with leadership—with leaders who model, advocate, and champion a parent-supportive culture. Policies alone are not enough if employees fear repercussions for using them. Training programs will fall flat if managers still reward availability over impact. The real shift happens when leaders set the example—when they take parental leave themselves, speak openly about the challenges and strengths of working parenthood, and design workplaces that enable parents to thrive rather than forcing them to compromise.

Every leader, from senior executives to frontline managers, must ask themselves: What kind of culture am I creating? What unspoken messages am I sending? Am I fostering a workplace where parents feel they can thrive?

The future belongs to companies that embrace parenthood as an asset rather than a liability. These companies will be the ones that attract the best talent, build the strongest leaders, and create workplaces that drive sustainable success.

This shift is not just about creating a "family-friendly" workplace—it is about redefining work itself. The skills that parenthood brings—resilience, crisis management, adaptability, empathy, and efficiency—are the very skills businesses need to succeed in an uncertain and fast-changing world.

The most successful companies of tomorrow will not be the ones that merely accommodate parents, but those that recognize, develop, and leverage the unique strengths that working parents bring to the table.

The path forward is clear:

- Build workplaces that make it possible for parents to thrive without sacrificing their careers.
- Redesign work to be more flexible, more human, and more results driven.
- Train leaders and managers to understand, support, and champion working parents.

- Celebrate parenthood as a leadership advantage, not a professional setback.

If we imagine the workplace of the future, it is one where no employee has to choose between being a great parent and being a great professional. It is a workplace where caregiving is not a career risk, but a career advantage. It is an organization where leadership development programs actively seek out and nurture the talents that parenthood builds. It is a culture where flexibility, inclusion, and innovation are the norms, not the exceptions.

The question for every business leader, every manager, and every organization is this: Will you be ahead of the curve, shaping the future of work? Or will you be left behind, clinging to outdated models that no longer serve the workforce of today?

The choice is yours. The time to act is now.

Final Thoughts: The Parenthood Advantage

Throughout this book, we've explored the ways parenthood shapes leadership, builds resilience, and drives workplace success. We've examined the history of parental leave, the challenges parents face, and the systemic changes needed to make work truly inclusive for caregivers. We've heard from employees and leaders who have navigated the intersection of career and parenthood, proving time and again that parenthood is not a limitation but rather an advantage.

Now, the responsibility falls on organizations to recognize and harness this advantage. To build workplaces where parents thrive. To create a future where no employee has to choose between their family and their ambition. To lead the way in making work more human, more inclusive, and more sustainable.

We strongly believe the parenthood advantage is a part of a larger shift in workplace dynamics. Many organizations are broadening their definition of inclusion. How organizations are able to structure more and more flexibility that will meet the needs of an increasingly diverse workforce is a challenge that will continue to grow and change. We think parents, who cross all groups, are at the center of this challenge.

The companies that do this will not only create better workplaces, they will create better businesses, better leaders, and a better future.

The parenthood advantage is real. The question is: Are you ready to embrace it?

Thank you for taking the time to engage with this book. The fact that you've made it to the end means you care deeply about building a workplace that truly supports and values parents—not just as employees, but as leaders.

None of this is easy. Shaping an inclusive, parent-supportive culture requires effort, commitment, and sometimes difficult conversations. It requires managers to think differently about leadership, teams to embrace new ways of working, and organizations to challenge long-standing norms about productivity and success. But as we've explored throughout this book, this work is not just necessary—it is essential.

If businesses are to thrive in the future of work, they must adapt. Supporting parents is not about making accommodations; it's about recognizing and leveraging the very skills that drive innovation, resilience, and leadership. It's about building workplaces that don't just attract talent but retain and develop it for long-term success.

If your organization is ready to take the next step in this journey, you don't have to do it alone. The Dagoba Group provides leadership development, coaching, and consulting to help organizations create truly inclusive workplaces. Whether you're looking for a book talk to introduce these ideas to your team, asynchronous or live leadership development, or coaching for managers and executives, we can help guide you through this transformation.

To learn more or to schedule a conversation, please reach out to us at Info@TheParenthoodAdvantage.com. The work ahead is important—and we are here to support you in making it a reality.

NOTES

Chapter 1

1. K. Donnelly, J. M.Twenge, M. A. Clark, S. K. Shaikh, A. Beiler-May, and N. T. Carter, "Attitudes Toward Women's Work and Family Roles in the United States, 1976–2013," *Psychology of Women Quarterly* 40(1) (2015): 1–14.

2. U.S. Bureau of Labor Statistics, *National Compensation Survey: Employee Benefits in the United States, March 2023—Family Leave Benefits* (U.S. Department of Labor, September 2023).

Chapter 2

1. C. Zimmermann, M. Krapf, and H. W. Ursprung, *Parenthood and Productivity of Highly Skilled Labor: Evidence from the Groves of Academe* (Federal Reserve Bank of St. Louis Working Paper 001A, 2014).

2. Michele K. Kacmar, Martha C. Andrews, Matthew Valle, C. Justice Tillman, and Cherray Clifton, "The Interactive Effects of Role Overload and Resilience on Family-Work Enrichment and Associated Outcomes," *The Journal of Social Psychology* 160, no. 5 (2020): 688–701.

3. LeanIn.org and McKinsey & Company, *Women in the Workplace 2022* (McKinsey & Company and LeanIn.org, 2022).

4. S. A. Hewlett, C. B. Luce, P. Shiller, and S. Southwell, *The Hidden Brain Drain: Off-Ramps and On-Ramps in Women's Careers* Report No. 9491 (Center for Work–Life Policy/Harvard Business Review Research, March 2005).

5. Work Institute, *2022 Retention Report: How Employers Caused the Great Resignation.* (Work Institute, 2022).

6. A. S. Modestino, J. J. Ladge, A. Swartz, and A. Lincoln, "Childcare Is a Business Issue," *Harvard Business Review*, April 29, 2021.

7. J. G. Grzywacz and A. M. Smith, "Work–Family Conflict and Health Among Working parents: Potential Linkages for Family Science and Social Neuroscience," *Family Relations* (2016).

8. Harter, Jim. "Employee Engagement on the Rise in the U.S." *Gallup News*, August 26, 2018.

9. Nicholas Bloom, *The Bright Future of Working from Home* (Stanford Institute for Economic Policy Research, June 2020).

10. Boston Consulting Group, Why Paid Family Leave Is Good Business (BCG, March 2017).

11. Emily Kos, Kelsey Clark, Nicole De Santis, and Tyler Joseph, *Childcare Benefits More Than Pay for Themselves at US Companies* (Boston Consulting Group, March 26, 2024).

12. World Economic Forum, *Global Gender Gap Report 2020* (World Economic Forum, 2020).

13. Lisa S. Kaplowitz and Kate Mangino, "Caregiver Employees Bring Unique Value to Companies," *Harvard Business Review*, August 10, 2023.

14. Ocejo, Michele. "The Role of Emotional Intelligence in Leadership." *The Secured Lender*, Secured Finance Network, March 7, 2025.

15. Hewlett, Luce, Shiller, and Southwell, *The Hidden Brain Drain.*

16. Bolden-Barrett, Valerie. "EY Says Its Female Turnover Dropped — Thanks in Part to Equal Leave for Dads." *HR Dive*, June 3, 2019.

17. Michelle J. Budig, *The Fatherhood Bonus and the Motherhood Penalty: Parenthood and the Gender Gap in Pay,* September 2, 2014, Third Way NEXT, Thirdway.org.

18. McKinsey & Company and LeanIn.org, *For Mothers in the Workplace, a Year—and Counting—Like No Other* (McKinsey & Company, 2020).

19. McKinsey & Company, *Diversity Wins: How Inclusion Matters* (McKinsey & Company, May 2020).

20. Nicholas Bloom, "Hybrid Work Is a Win-Win-Win for Companies, Workers, and the Environment," *Stanford Report*, June 25, 2024.

21. Aliss Higham, "Gen Z Ranks Work-Life Balance Over Pay: Research," *Newsweek*, January 21, 2025.

22. Accenture, *Impact of Extended Maternity Leave on Employee Retention*, company internal report, cited in "Paid Parental Leave: How Much Time Is Enough?," *New America's Better Life Lab* (2023).

23. AARP Public Policy Institute and National Alliance for Caregiving, *Caregiving in the U.S.* (AARP and National Alliance for Caregiving, 2015).

24. Boston Consulting Group, *Why Paid Family Leave Is Good Business* (BCG, February 7, 2017).

25. The Ohio State University Office of the Chief Wellness Officer, *Examining the Epidemic of Working Parental Burnout and Strategies to Help* (Ohio State University Office of the Chief Wellness Officer and College of Nursing, May 2022).

Chapter 3

1. Lisa Giuliano, David I. Levine, and Jonathan Leonard, "Manager Race and the Race of New Hires," *Journal of Labor Economics* 27, no. 4 (2009).

2. Shelley J. Correll, Stephen Benard, and In Paik, "Getting a Job: Is There a Motherhood Penalty?" *American Journal of Sociology* 112, no. 5 (2007).

3. Deloitte Global, *Women @ Work: A Global Outlook* (Deloitte, 2023–2024).

4. McKinsey & Company and LeanIn.org. *Women in the Workplace 2022* (McKinsey & Company and LeanIn.org, 2022).

5. Claire Cain Miller, "A Child Helps Your Career, if You're a Man," *The New York Times*, September 6, 2014.

6. Bernhard Stellner, "Effects of Fatherhood on Leadership Behaviour of Managers," *International Journal of Organizational Leadership* 10 (2021).

7. L. A. Rudman and K. Mescher, "Penalizing Men Who Request a Family Leave: Is Flexibility Stigma a Femininity Stigma?," *Journal of Social Issues* 69(2) (2013).

8. Dominique Goldschmitt, "What's It Like Being Childfree at Work?," SHRM, June 8, 2022.

9. ResumeLab. *Childfree at Work: The Stigma, Stereotypes, and Benefits of Being Childless in the Workplace.* Survey Report. June 2022.

10. J. H. Pencavel, *Diminishing Returns at Work: The Consequence of Long Working Hours* (Oxford University Press, 2018).

Chapter 4

1. Hongjian Cao, W Roger Mills-Koonce, Claire Wood, and Mark A. Fine, "Identity Transformation During the Transition to Parenthood Among Same-Sex Couples: An Ecological, Stress-Strategy-Adaptation Perspective," *Journal of Family Theory & Review* 8, no. 1 (2016): 30.

2. A. E. Goldberg and M. Perry-Jenkins, "Division of Labor and Working-Class Women's Well-Being Across the Transition to Parenthood," *Journal of Family Psychology* 18(1) (2004): 225–236.

3. S. L. Katz-Wise, H. A. Priess, and J. S. Hyde, "Gender-Role Attitudes and Behavior Across the Transition to Parenthood," *Developmental Psychology* 46(1) (2010): 18–28.

4. K. K. Bost, M. J. Cox, M. R. Burchinal, and C. Payne, "Structural and Supportive Changes in Couples' Family and Friendship Networks across the Transition to Parenthood," *Journal of Marriage and Family* 64(2) (2002): 517–531.

5. Pew Research Center, *Raising Kids and Running a Household: How Working Parents Share the Load* (Pew Research Center, November 4, 2015).

6. Rachel Muller-Heyndyk, "Becoming a Parent Boosts Work Performance," *HR Magazine*, October 25, 2019.

7. Brené Brown, *Daring Greatly: How the Courage to Be Vulnerable Transforms the Way We Live, Love, Parent, and Lead* (Gotham Books, 2012).

8. Centers for Disease Control and Prevention, *Improving Maternal Mental Health Care: Program in Support of Moms (PRISM)* (Centers for Disease Control and Prevention, 2024).

9. Mahalia Mayne, "Third of Working Parents Struggling with Severe Stress, Study Finds," *People Management*, January 14, 2025.

10. Mayne, "Third of Working Parents."

11. Amanda Barroso, *For American Couples, Gender Gaps in Sharing Household Responsibilities Persist Amid Pandemic* (Pew Research Center, January 25, 2021).

12. McKinsey & Company, *A Fresh Look at Paternity Leave: Why the Benefits Extend beyond the Personal* (McKinsey & Company, March 5, 2021).

Chapter 5

1. Ioana Lupu and Mayra Ruiz-Castro, "Work-Life Balance Is a Cycle, Not an Achievement," *Harvard Business Review*, January 29, 2021.

2. Megan Leonhardt, "Millions of Working Mothers in the U.S. Are Suffering from Burnout," CNBC, December 3, 2020.

3. John H. Pencavel, *The Productivity of Working Hours*, IZA Discussion Paper No. 8129, April 2014.

4. Jen Fisher, Jay Bhatt, and Amy Fields, "Six Leader/Worker Disconnects Affecting Workplace Well-Being," *Deloitte Insights,* November 14, 2023.

5. Slack, "Swap Long Video Calls and Emails for Asynchronous Video." *Slack* Blog, July 22, 2022.

6. Society for Human Resource Management (SHRM), *The State of Global Workplace Culture: Burnout, Search Intent, and Engagement* [PDF] (Society for Human Resource Management, 2024).

7. Nicholas Bloom, James Liang, John Roberts, and Zhichun Jenny Ying, *Does Working from Home Work? Evidence from a Chinese Experiment,* Working Paper No. 18871 (National Bureau of Economic Research, 2013).

8. Gallup, *The Remote Work Paradox: Engaged and Distressed* (Gallup, 2023).

Chapter 6

1. American Psychiatric Association. "Lifestyle to Support Mental Health." Accessed August 17, 2025.

Chapter 7

1. Travis Bradberry, "Why Emotional Intelligence Can Boost Your Career and Save Your Life," TalentSmartEQ, June 20, 2022.

Chapter 8

1. National Partnership for Women & Families, *Paid Family and Medical Leave Is Good for Business* (fact sheet, National Partnership for Women & Families, Washington, DC, May 2025).

2. A. Gaston, S. A., Edwards, and J. A. Tober, "Parental Leave and Child Care Arrangements During the First 12 Months of Life Are Associated with Children's Development Five Years Later," *International Journal of Child, Youth and Family Studies* 6 (2) (2015).

INDEX